DESIGNING
MULTIMEDIA

DESIGNING
MULTIMEDIA

A VISUAL GUIDE TO MULTIMEDIA
AND ONLINE GRAPHIC DESIGN

LISA LOPUCK

PEACHPIT PRESS

DESIGNING MULTIMEDIA

Lisa Lopuck

Peachpit Press
2414 Sixth Street
Berkeley, CA 94710
800-283-9444
510-548-4393
510-548-5991 (fax)

Find us on the World Wide Web at: http://www.peachpit.com
Peachpit Press is a division of Addison-Wesley Publishing Company

Editor: Liz Sizensky
Cover design: Lisa Lopuck
Interior design and illustration: Lisa Lopuck
Production: Lisa Lopuck

ISBN 0-201-88398-8

0 9 8 7 6 5 4 3 2 1

Printed and bound in the United States of America

This book is dedicated, with great thanks and respect, to my UCLA design professor, Bill Brown, who first introduced me to multimedia.

ACKNoWLEDGMENTS

INDIVIDUALS

I owe special thanks to the following people for their friendship, support, and advice:

Liz Sizensky
Ted Nace
Roslyn Bullas
Bill Brown
Steve Gano
Kristee Rosendahl
Abbe Don
Nathan Shedroff
Judy Genovese
Matt Gunnell
The staff of the San Francisco State
   University Multimedia Studies Program

COMPANIES

Artwork and multimedia titles featured in this book have been reproduced with the permission of the following companies:

American Center for Design	Living Books
Ameritech	Maeght Foundation
Apple Computer	Oakland Museum
Bastide and Bastide	PowerTV
C-Wave	Presto Studios
Cyan	Real World Multimedia
Dan Design	Sierra On-Line
Dorling Kindersley	Sumeria
Humongous Entertainment	Sunburst Communications
HyperBole Studios	2Market Inc.
Interactive Factory	vivid studios
I/O 360 Design	World Lithographic Services
Kaleida Labs	Zenda Studio
KidSoft	

CoNTENTS

CONTENTS

CoNTENTS

F⌀REWORD

Ten years ago, you could count on one hand the number of "traditional" designers who had made the leap onto the computer. Over the years, more accessible and usable digital tools have been made available to a growing computer design community. While many designers will continue to use these tools and computers to generate traditional print materials, other designers want to make the leap onto a new playing field—designing interactive interfaces for kiosks, presentations, multimedia products, and online services.

The quality of the design of these digital products is now acknowledged as a major key to a product's success. Because of this, the designer now has a major role to play, not only as an implementer, but also as a source for ideas and concepts. Professional designers in a range of fields—graphics, industrial design, and architecture—are now being called upon to conceptualize, design, and implement products for a different kind of display, the screen. This screen, whether from a computer, TV, or handheld display, is a "portal" on a world that is anything but flat; it's dynamic, multisensory, and pliable.

Because of this, designers currently working in this field will generally tell you that while they call upon and use many of their traditional design skills and aesthetics, designing an interactive experience is essentially a new challenge. We take classes, go to conferences, talk with peers, buy books, and join organizations in an attempt to educate ourselves as fast and as thoroughly as we can. This can be frustrating, and, in truth, the newness of interactive design as a profession and as an industry has made it difficult to uncover answers to our questions. How do we make the leap? How do we think and build for this new medium?

I met Lisa Lopuck in 1991, when I was Senior Designer at Apple Computer's Multimedia Lab in San Francisco, California. Her enthusiasm and willingness to explore multimedia technologies and her own sense of design made it apparent that she would be among those designers able to bridge the gap to multimedia. I am delighted to be a small part of her book because I think it helps others make that leap.

Designing Multimedia deals with some of the issues designers encounter when conceptualizing and modeling an interactive experience. It encompasses some of the notions of how to structure information, how to anticipate user experience, and how to generate visually compelling interfaces. Lisa has laid out, in a highly visual and accessible manner, ways for us to understand both the process of multimedia design and the tools needed to accomplish our visions.

I applaud her never-ending enthusiasm and her effort to communicate this information to a growing group of design professionals who are excited about this medium and who yearn for more knowledge about how to think (and feel) about designing with bits.

—KRISTEE ROSENDAHL

IS THIS BOOK FOR YOU?

Increasingly, graphic designers, artists, and other creative professionals are being asked to design interactive multimedia titles and Web sites. Many times after taking the assignment, however, designers realize that they are in over their heads when dealing with technical issues, color palettes, and production processes. Multimedia and online design have become their own specialties—requiring that creative professionals understand these new media landscapes.

Designing Multimedia presents a holistic "soup-to-nuts" approach that includes the multimedia production process; the technology; user interface design; graphic production tips, strategies, and exercises; and color and palettes—all intended to get you started designing multimedia. The information is presented in a clear, down-to-earth, visual style—a style just for visual people.

This book grew out of a class I teach at the San Francisco State University Multimedia Studies Program, "Graphic Design: Making the Transition to Multimedia," and so it has been field-tested by a variety of talented and established designers. I hope that you will find this book as instrumental as they did.

—LISA LOPUCK

CHAPTER 1

MULTIMEDIA
IN A NUTSHELL

This chapter takes a look at the multimedia creation process step by step, from brainstorming to final testing. Each step is presented from a clear "bird's-eye view" so that you may begin to understand the creative process and think strategically about how to organize information for multimedia.

Sleep is for beginners.

—Ken Fromm, vivid studios

INTR⌀DUCTION

WHAT IS MULTIMEDIA ANYWAY?

Multimedia is a collection of various media—video, sound, graphics, animation, and text—that come together to form a single unit. Interactive multimedia means that all of these media are structured in such a way that the audience has control over their presentation. The designer's job is to coalesce this variety of elements into a united structure that is both easy to use and greater than the sum of its parts. This last point is especially important. Multimedia for multimedia's sake is just an expensive exercise. There needs to be real value achieved through the use of multimedia, a value that independent media alone cannot provide.

SPECIALIZING IN MULTIMEDIA GRAPHIC DESIGN

In the early days of the multimedia industry, the pool of professional designers who specialized in multimedia was a relatively small one. To compensate, the industry made use of "backyard" designers. Just as in the early days of computer desktop publishing, non-designers from the technical side of multimedia had a great time with some powerful design tools and became instant, self-styled "multimedia graphic designers"—some even made a living at it!

Today's climate is much different. The ante is up. As the industry matures and as more powerful machines appear on the market, audiences are demanding the high level of polish that only skilled, talented people can provide. Not just any designer, however, can jump in to work on a multimedia title. Just as product design, industrial design, and packaging design are specialty areas, each presenting a unique set of problems, materials, and design considerations, so, too, is multimedia design. This book discusses the tools and technology, as well as the pitfalls and other issues, that you need to be familiar with before embarking on a multimedia design project. Beyond that, this book teaches designers how to understand multimedia as a medium. Like any other art form, you need to have an intimate understanding of your material before you can best design for it.

UNDERSTANDING THE MEDIUM

What we know today as "interactive multimedia" is a single form. Its structure is the result of the combination of the software that physically holds it together, the ergonomics of user interaction, and finally, the message. Choice of software and innovative user interface design have profound effects on the final product. Once you understand how software

Individual media elements, such as sound and video, need to be specially prepared before they can be included in interactive multimedia titles.

and user interface affect multimedia, you can create a multimedia structure that best communicates your message.

CREATIVE THINKING FOR MULTIMEDIA

Perhaps the biggest hurdle for creative people coming into multimedia from other fields is the realization that their skills are only one piece of the puzzle. Often, after years of focusing on one medium, it is easy to neglect other media that can come into play. For instance, my background is in the silent world of 2-D illustration and design, so I need to remind myself to incorporate sound in my multimedia projects.

In general, creative people who have a wide and varied interest in media of all kinds are ripe for multimedia. However, it is important to have a focus. People who say they can do video, sound, and a little programming indicate that not only do they lack understanding of the intricacies of those areas, but they also are probably not very good at any of them. In my opinion, a jack of all trades is a master of none.

In addition, because multimedia provides so much depth of content—so many facets of information presented through various media—the best multimedia designers are those who are extremely organized and good at categorizing information. It is important not to get bogged down with all the little details; the more you can step back and view the whole abstract picture, the better off you are.

Designers at the French company Bastide and Bastide used a video "walk-through" of the Maeght Foundation's sculpture garden as the primary user interface for *The Maeght Foundation: A Stroll in 20th Century Art*. As a result, this Macromedia Director-based multimedia title is dynamic and content-rich, yet elegant in its simplicity (see pages 126–127 for more about this title).

THE PEOPLE

Much like the film industry, multimedia production involves numerous people, each of whom brings a unique skill into the mix yet understands enough about every other team member's task so that there is a sense of mutual respect and communication. This is a tall order because multimedia is quite a production, and knowing a little about all aspects, plus becoming an expert in one area, takes time and experience.

Today's multimedia project does not always have the focus or budget to include all of the following people, but it will include a subset that is particular to the project's needs. Depending on the focus of the project, any of the following professionals may end up playing the most important role.

GRAPHIC DESIGNERS

Many times the graphic designer is also the art director and production artist rolled into one. Larger projects, however, generally require some sort of design team. In that situation, the creative director or art director spends a lot of time with the producer and reports back to the design team. In any case, it is important to include designers in the initial conceptual discussions of a multimedia project because they are the ones who know how to organize and communicate visual information.

PROGRAMMERS

The programmer and the designer must get along very well because these two form the most basic team unit and are always working hand in hand to realize one vision. It is imperative to find a programmer with multimedia experience. An engineer with a software application background speaks very different user interface and structural languages.

PRODUCERS

Multimedia producers generally handle the day-to-day management of people and finances. They handle all the business aspects of a project, including client relations, and work with the project manager to ensure that all elements of a project come together on time and within budget.

PROJECT MANAGERS

Project managers are responsible for overseeing the project's timeline and resources. This job can be a three-ring circus because nothing

▲

Multimedia composer and sound designer Anthony Hoffer developed award-winning sound and original music for Sumeria's *Ocean Life IV: The Great Barrier Reef.*

ever goes as planned, and the project manager must shift resources and priorities around to keep the project under control. Because project managers supervise the daily process and allocate resources, they provide helpful insights when it comes to putting multimedia proposals together.

WRITERS

Creative and technical writers may be needed to develop everything from characters and stories to polished, effective text. Writing for multimedia presents its own set of problems. For example, what does it mean to create stories in which the writer does not have express control over the flow or outcome? Also, because of the limited screen space, writers for multimedia need a concise writing style.

USER INTERFACE DESIGNERS

Tradition in the computer software industry has carved out user interface design as a separate profession. However, I think the basic principles of communication design and industrial design are close cousins to the art of user interface design. Therefore, communication and industrial designers can easily transfer their skills into user interface design (see Chapter 4, "User Interface Design").

SOUND DESIGNERS

Well-executed voice-overs, original compositions, and vibrant sound effects designed expressly for a multimedia environment do wonders for a title. Creating sound for such a nonlinear environment as multimedia, however, not only requires an understanding of the interworkings of digital audio but also an intimate understanding of the architecture of multimedia. For instance, user interaction sometimes requires the use of sound loops or multiple sound channels to attain virtually "continuous" sound.

VIDEOGRAPHERS

Because video, like sound, is inherently linear, the same careful planning and creative thinking goes into every "megabyte" of multimedia video. Some artists, like Greg Roach, have invented ways to create interactive video stories, while others have successfully integrated traditional techniques, such as cutaways.

3-D AND 2-D ANIMATORS

Multimedia usually involves animation of some sort. It may be as simple as the creation of "highlight" states (graphics that acknowledge a user's action) or as complex as developing entire worlds and characters and bringing them to life.

Writer and designer Larry Kay worked with the core team of Humongous Entertainment to develop *Freddi Fish and the Case of the Missing Kelp Seeds*, a remarkably interactive adventure game.

TﬂMELINE

Below is a media production schedule used by KidSoft in the development of a quarterly CD-ROM. Time moves along from left to right, while projects are stacked down the left column. On the right, blocks of time are highlighted for each project.

Throughout the creation of a multimedia title, a timeline is an invaluable reference tool. Updated schedules should be continually circulated to team members so that everyone has an overhead view of where they are in the process. There are two kinds of timelines presented on these pages, a media production schedule (used by project managers to coordinate the various development efforts) and a timeline showing, in broad strokes, the overall multimedia design and development process.

MEDIA PRODUCTION TIMELINE

What does the media production schedule of multimedia look like? If you were to draw a diagram of a multimedia title's workflow, it would look quite staggered. Some media are produced simultaneously while other production overlaps. In all cases, some media will be dependent on the completion of other media. This creates a domino effect and is generally the single largest reason for a slipping schedule.

Project managers develop and keep track of the timeline (see example at left). They are responsible for scheduling all the production efforts into a realistic time frame. Realistic means taking into account the

inevitable delays and creating a timeline flexible enough to allow for changes along the way. For instance, it may be a good idea to work out worst-case and best-case scenarios and keep both on hand as your guides.

CREATING PRODUCTION TIMELINES

Before you can create a schedule you need to have a fairly detailed "paper design" (see pages 14–15). From this document, you can derive a master "to do" list of all the media production necessary for the project.

By understanding the complexity involved in each production area, you can map out realistic blocks of time for every one of them. Then, point out which media are dependent on the completion of other media and start arranging these blocks of time accordingly.

OVERALL MULTIMEDIA TIMELINE

The timeline at right gives an overall picture of the entire multimedia process. I have broken it down into two areas: the design phase and the development phase. The design phase encompasses all the initial steps, from brainstorming and storyboarding to the creation and user testing of the prototype. The development stage is broken down into a few subphases: media production, alpha, beta, and finally, golden master. Each of these phases is explained later in this chapter, but they are presented here so that you can see where they fall on the timeline.

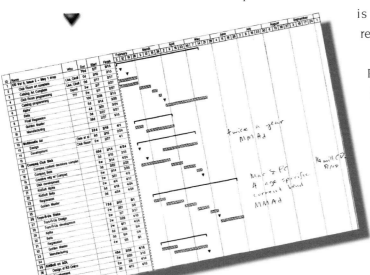

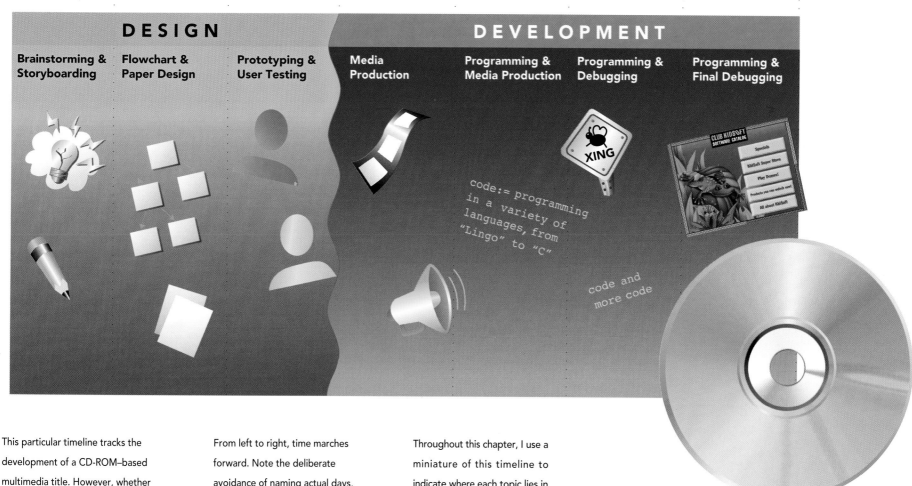

Approximately 10% complete (begin paper design)

Approximately 20% complete (begin prototype)

Approximately 30% complete (begin development)

Approximately 40% complete (begin programming)

Approximately 65% complete (alpha stage)

Approximately 80% complete (beta stage)

100% complete (golden master)

DESIGN

DEVELOPMENT

Brainstorming & Storyboarding

Flowchart & Paper Design

Prototyping & User Testing

Media Production

Programming & Media Production

Programming & Debugging

Programming & Final Debugging

code:= programming in a variety of languages, from "Lingo" to "C"

code and more code

XING

CLUB KIDSOFT SOFTWARE CATALOG

This particular timeline tracks the development of a CD-ROM–based multimedia title. However, whether the delivery medium is a CD-ROM, a stand-alone kiosk, interactive television, or online, this timeline is a reflection of the basic multimedia design and development process.

From left to right, time marches forward. Note the deliberate avoidance of naming actual days, weeks, or months. Multimedia projects can take anywhere from four months, as in the case of KidSoft's quarterly CD-ROM, to a year or more to produce.

Throughout this chapter, I use a miniature of this timeline to indicate where each topic lies in the production process.

BRAINST⊕RMING

DESIGN **DEVELOPMENT**

The first steps on the timeline are brainstorming and storyboarding. These initial parts of the design phase can take anywhere from a couple of days to a couple of weeks.

The first question that should be raised when planning a multimedia project is who is the audience? Age, sex, and nationality have a big impact on all aspects of the design of a multimedia title, from user interface to graphic design and structure. The next issue to keep in mind is why multimedia? Is this yet another arbitrary use of multimedia? Or, is there some real value achieved by using multimedia for this project, a value that wouldn't be possible through other, more traditional media?

Keeping the above two issues in mind, it's time to break out the white board and start brainstorming. To me, brainstorming involves a tight group of about three to seven key people, including a designer, a programmer, and anyone else important to the particular project. More than seven people in these initial conceptual meetings can be cumbersome, because managing each other's thoughts and criticisms takes time away from the free flow of ideas. This is a time to present all ideas, good and bad alike, without judgment. Sometimes what are thought of at first as the worst ideas evolve into a unique contribution down the line.

MARKETING AND DISTRIBUTION

If you are designing a commercial product, now is the time to begin your marketing and distribution plans. It may seem early, but it can take months to resolve these issues. Most often, the difference between a hit title and a dud is not content, but actually getting shelf space in the stores!

The initial typography sketch for Courtney Lane, Julie Gant, and Lisa Lopuck's UCLA student project, *The Monarch Butterfly*, set the creative tone for the final product.

SToRYBOARDING

Initial storyboards for a title do not have to be anything fancy, or even accurate, for that matter. They simply serve the purpose of roughly illustrating a concept and inspiring people to think of the possibilities. I like to create what I call "one-pagers" for each title concept. They are one- to two-page write-ups consisting of three sketches per page (see sample storyboard for *Expedition Earth* on the following pages). This way, I can generate a large repertoire of ideas in a relatively short amount of time.

Storyboards should showcase all the key screens, or "places" (see sidebar at right), that comprise the proposed title. Each screen is accompanied by brief text describing the scene and the user interaction, as well as any dynamics, including sound.

Brainstorming and storyboarding are critical phases of a title's development. It is at this point that a title's creators have the first thoughts about how to structure content and how users will interact with it. Therefore, it is crucial to have a designer involved at this stage. All too often, designers are called on at production time for "cosmetics." However, multimedia designers are more like architects—able to design sound structures as well as make them aesthetically pleasing.

PLACeS

The concept of "places" is a good way to think about the organization of a multimedia title. Many people think of multimedia in terms of "screen shots"—single frames used to show the look and feel of a title. However, those screen shots are only partially representative of the whole experience. Screen shots only present a static page. A static page is a comfortable, contained environment to design, but page design is a bad metaphor for designing multimedia. Multimedia, like film, is not static. It occurs in a dynamic space and is always changing over time.

Therefore, a better way to think about multimedia is as a series of environments, or "places." For instance, imagine a house as a multimedia title. There are many places within the house: bedrooms, bathrooms, a kitchen, etc. Each serves a different function and is where different activities can occur. A snapshot of each room only gives an *impression* of what happens there.

When conceptualizing a multimedia project, you need to think about all the different places that you will need to accommodate the given content. Then, illustrate the action in each place in a series of storyboards.

SAMPLE STORYBOARD: EXPEDITION EARTH

An archaeological learning adventure series, which takes you to the ends of the earth to discover its secrets.

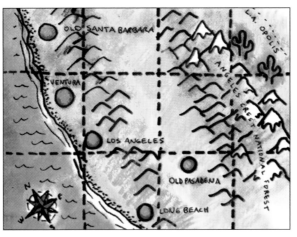

For millions of years, animals, dinosaurs, and more recently, humans, have traversed the balmy lands of what is now L.A. Opolis, leaving behind countless clues that enable scientists to glance into their daily lives.

Unlock the historical secrets of the Southern California coastline as you and a team of archaeologists search for lost treasures, creatures, and cultures on this edition of *Expedition Earth*.

Play against your friends as if you were competing teams of archaeologists. Watch your budget—you can run out of money before finding anything of interest, and there goes next season's digs! However, if you do find something, the university just may extend your time and budget.

Choose a sector from our map outlining the major cities of twentieth-century Los Angeles. Each sector is broken down in a traditional grid system. If you are lucky, you'll choose a section rich with valuable artifacts, revealing clues about ancient civilizations or extinct animals! If you are not lucky, you could be digging for quite a while. It's up to you to spend your time and money wisely.

Wow, a discovery already! The first layer is pretty easy—just a bunch of stuff left from the big quake of 2001. Keep searching; you never know when something of value will turn up.

As you go, you need to determine the approximate age of each layer. This way, you can more easily decipher what it is you actually find and what it is worth.

As you dig deeper through the layers of time, put the bones and artifacts you encounter into special collection bins for later analysis. Eureka! You've found an entire skeleton of an animal. This could be too good to be true; better take it over to the lab right away. Who knows, you might be on to something big.

When you are ready to analyze some of your findings, take them over to the lab. Here you can carbon-date each object to zero in on the exact time frame of your findings. Then, you can begin to identify your artifacts, by looking them up in our handy online reference guide or by consulting the experts.

Ah ha! That full skeleton you found is just a common horse. How old is it? How big was it when it was alive? Use your measuring tools to find out.

Let's create a timeline of all your findings. Hey, this is a nice item to include in your museum exhibit along with all your artifacts.

Make a compelling presentation to the university when you think you have a good collection of stuff, and you just might edge out your competitors for that museum exhibit.

FL⦾WCHARTS

DESIGN | **DEVELOPMENT**

Next in the design phase is the development of a flowchart. A flowchart complements the storyboards by giving a sense of organization and navigation to a multimedia design concept.

While a storyboard paints the initial picture of a multimedia concept, a flowchart gives a sense of its structure and user interaction. The flowchart begins to "wire" together all the places mentioned in the storyboards.

There are a number of strategies you can use to organize multimedia content. Of the possibilities, a hierarchical system is perhaps one of the simplest organizational strategies. The flowchart at right shows the hierarchy used in KidSoft's quarterly CD-ROM magazine and software catalog for kids. By clicking on one of three buttons on the main screen, users go to either the "Clubroom" (for kids to play in), the "Catalog" (for adults to browse through software products), or the "Buy Now" screen (for purchasing products). In turn, each of these three screens has buttons that branch into other areas.

When organizing multimedia, think of the environments, or "places," you will need in order to communicate your message. Chances are that you will have multiple places, so you need to think about how each place relates to the others. For instance, imagine that you create a 3-D virtual ocean to swim in, but you would like to examine the things you encounter in a separate lablike place. How do you connect those two very different places? What structural and user interface conventions make the most sense? A flowchart helps you sketch out the answers.

Chapter 2, "The Architecture of Multimedia," explores a variety of multimedia structures that will help you think about new ways to organize information.

The cover screen branches to three different places: the "Clubroom" (accessible by clicking on the armchair), the "Catalog," and the "Buy Now" screen.

The "Clubroom" is the kids' activity area of the CD.

From the "Clubroom," kids zoom in on various activities, such as contests.

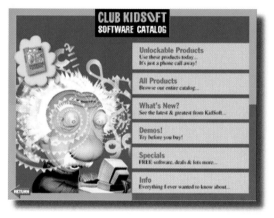

KidSoft's electronic catalog interface allows you to browse, sort, demo, and buy kids' multimedia software.

Clicking on a product brings up more information (see below).

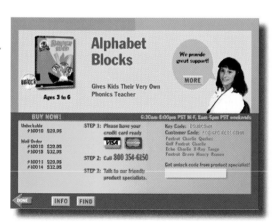

The "Buy Now" screen is accessible from the cover screen and from within the "Catalog."

THe PAPER DeSIGN

DESIGN DEVELOPMENT

▲

At this point in the design phase, the paper design is developed. This essential document will act as a blueprint for the entire project's development.

Once you have created a series of storyboards and preliminary flowcharts, it is time to work through, on paper and in fine detail, the logistics of a title. The "paper design," as I call it, is the "blueprint" for a multimedia title. It covers the structural design and the software strategy, as well as the media production requirements and the user interface design. Paper designs generally consist of the following documents: the original storyboards, a flowchart indicating the architectural structure and general navigation through the title, and a detailed "functional spec."

FUNCTIONAL SPEC

The functional spec walks through each scenario of the title, frame by frame, detailing the action on the screen and illustrating how the user interacts with it. For example, when a character walks across the screen, the user interaction specs may state "when mouse rolls within character's shape, then character reacts to user in such-and-such a way" and "if user clicks on character, then character does such-and-such." The same holds true for describing "buttons" (buttons are "hot" areas on the screen that the user may click in order to trigger an action). For example, "if mouse rolls over button, then button displays its 'highlight' state. If user clicks on button, then button displays its 'clicked' state." The functional spec also names the various media (sound, video, animation, graphics, etc.) used for each screen.

Graphics used to map out each frame for a functional spec do not need to be specific. In fact, the more abstract the better, because that allows you to concentrate on the actual function being illustrated.

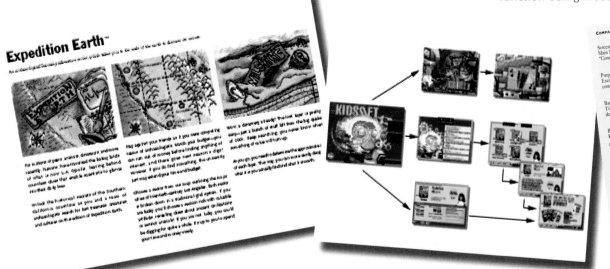

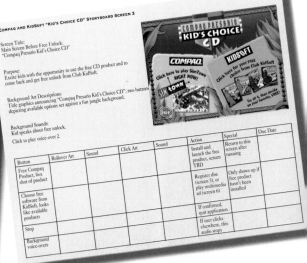

This example is from the functional spec for the *Compaq Presario Kid's Choice CD*.

It is important to develop a working title of each screen plus a brief description of its purpose.

Brief descriptions of both the background art and the sound requirements are mentioned.

COMPAQ AND KIDSOFT "KID'S CHOICE CD" STORYBOARD SCREEN 3

Screen Title:
Main Screen Before Free Unlock.
"Compaq Presario Kid's Choice CD"

Purpose:
Excite kids with the opportunity to use the free CD product and to come back and get free unlock from Club KidSoft.

Background Art Descriptions:
Title graphics announcing "Compaq Presario Kid's Choice CD"; two buttons depicting available options set against a fun jungle background.

Background Sounds:
Kid speaks about free unlock.

Click to play voice-over 2.

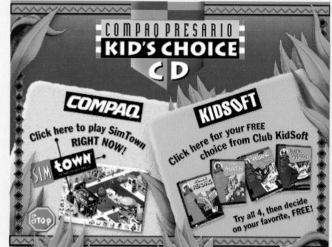

In this case, the design was already determined. Ordinarily, this space would show either a storyboard sketch or a simple diagram that "blocks" out the necessary design components.

KidSoft uses a graph to itemize buttons and their functions. This is intended only as an example; you should develop your own ways to itemize media—whatever makes the most sense to you. For example, you could organize by media type—animation, sound, graphics, etc.

Button	Rollover Art	Sound	Click Art	Sound	Action	Special	Due Date
Free Compaq Product, box shot of product					Install and launch the free product, screen TBD	Return to this screen after running	
Choose free software from KidSoft, looks like available products					Register disc (screen 5), or play multimedia ad (screen 6)	Only shows up if free product hasn't been installed	
Stop					If confirmed, quit application		
Background voice-overs					If user clicks elsewhere, this audio stops		

TH*e* PR**o**TOTYPE

The final part of the design phase is dedicated to prototyping and testing a multimedia concept to get real-world feedback.

Once a functional spec is complete and the creative ideas are well established, it is time to start prototyping. A prototype will confirm whether or not your storyboards and paper design are sound. There is nothing like seeing all of your thoughts, ideas, and solutions in action to point out both their brilliance and their flaws.

There are a number of ways to approach creating a prototype. One way is to use a friendly authoring tool, such as Macromedia Director, for the sole purpose of mocking up the user interaction and the graphic style (authoring tools are software packages used to "wire" media together in order to create a multimedia title). This tool does not necessarily need to be the one you use for the final product; it simply serves to put together a quick prototype for initial user testing (see sidebar at right). The drawback is that you may spend a week or more creating something that will eventually be thrown away. In addition, each authoring tool performs differently, so you must take those differences into account, both when testing and when creating the final product.

Another approach is to pick a small cross section of the title and use your intended authoring tool to put together a prototype. This gives you the opportunity to see if your authoring tool is well suited for what you want to accomplish. For example, some authoring tools are better at handling animation, while others are better at database functions (see Chapter 3, "A Look at Authoring Tools"). The benefit of this way of prototyping is that much of the effort expended on the prototype can carry over to the final production stage.

As I mentioned on page 6, the prototype is considered part of the design phase. This means that any last-minute changes in user interface, graphic design, or structure need to be made now, because after this we move into the development phase.

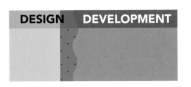

The interim design phase introduced a road metaphor. Not only does this create a more dynamic space, but it also helps to organize the information more clearly—the user is not overwhelmed by choices. In addition, the road metaphor reinforces the idea of a "journey" through a historic past.

Voices of the 30s, published by WINGS for Learning/ Sunburst Communications, was originally designed for a small black-and-white screen accompanied by a laserdisc. For subsequent versions, the decision was made to integrate the interface and video into one CD-ROM product.

In the final design, the hierarchy is "flattened" from two levels to one (see "Hierarchy," pages 22–23). Every section is accessible from the main interface screen. Also, each billboard's image becomes the background for its section, giving users a consistent "sense of place."

USeR TESTiNG

User testing is an extremely important exercise that should occur throughout the design and development process. A few hours spent testing your prototype with a focus group (a group of randomly selected people who represent your target market) can save hundreds of production hours later on.

Structural and user interface decisions are made by people who really understand multimedia, how it works, and how to navigate through it. Once a design team becomes intimate with a project, it is easy for them to take its structure and user interface for granted. A fresh look at the project, especially by someone who is less familiar with multimedia, will quickly tell you what makes sense and what doesn't. This person helps you gauge if the product is understandable to a mass audience.

It is a good idea to videotape a user test because you may not remember everything said or every reaction. Also, and perhaps most importantly, video captures the context of a user's reaction. One pitfall to videotaping, however, is that some users are intimidated by the camera and will be more reserved with their feedback.

FiNAL PRoDUCTION

DESIGN | DEVELOPMENT

The development stage begins with the production of final media; when a good portion of it is completed, initial programming may begin. From then on, three milestones mark the final production efforts: alpha, beta, and golden master.

PRODUCING FINAL MEDIA

The development phase begins with final media production. Graphics, animation, sound, video, etc., must be developed, at least to some extent, so that programmers may begin to integrate them into a framework. An alternative to waiting for final media is to use "stand-in" media. Sometimes, however, it takes longer than expected to create effective stand-ins, so time is often better spent creating final media. In any event, the various media need to be prepared in multimedia-specific ways. There are standard formats and limitations for every medium, from video to graphics. Chapter 5, "Graphic Production Tips and Strategies," covers the specifics of producing graphics for multimedia.

The development phase is the home stretch—all media production is coordinated for optimal efficiency. At this point, even the simplest re-design has a tendency to ripple back, adversely affecting other production areas.

PROGRAMMING

Using an authoring tool (see Chapter 3, "A Look at Authoring Tools"), a programmer can begin to assemble all the media into the structure that's been determined by the paper design. Programming continues until the entire initial framework is put together. When all the "places to go and things to do" are up and running, a multimedia title is what is called "feature complete" and is ready to enter the alpha stage.

ALPHA

Being feature complete is a requirement before multimedia can be considered "in alpha." Alpha is testing time, so it is important that everything that will be incorporated into the title is readily accessible by the testers. There should not be any "bugs" (malfunctions) that block access to the major features or places of the title.

Quality assurance, or "Q.A.," testers go through the alpha version of the title with a fine-tooth comb and keep track of any bugs they encounter—where they happen and what causes them. All the while, programming and media production are still charging forward. Updated versions of the project go back and forth from the programmers to the testers until all the major "crashing bugs" have been weeded out. (Crashing bugs are the ones so severe that they literally freeze up, or crash, the computer.) With no more crashing

CLUB KIDSOFT
SOFTWARE CATALOG

Specials

KidSoft Super Store

Play Demos!

Products you can unlock now!

All about KidSoft

Aside from CD-ROM mastering, CDs are excellent archives for source media.

bugs, a multimedia title is ready to enter "beta."

Beta

The beta stage is the last round of final media production, programming, and testing before a title is declared finished and ready for duplication. At this point, there should be only minor bugs left in the title. These stragglers need to be prioritized and handled accordingly, otherwise this fine-tuning process can drag on indefinitely.

Golden master

At last, after months of planning, producing, and testing, the project is nearly perfect. Any minute bugs will be removed in the next release (if at all), and it is time to cut the master CD-ROM—the golden master. From this disc all the rest are pressed, then packaged and distributed.

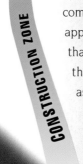

DeBUGGING

The complexity of an interactive multimedia endeavor almost ensures that there will be "bugs." Authoring tools are being pushed to their limits, multiple media elements need to be coordinated, and all of it needs to perform on today's lowest-common-denominator computers.

Bugs are everything from major malfunctions that crash the computer to minor problems like having the wrong font size appear in a text window. Bugs are generally so numerous that they need to be methodically categorized according to their severity and importance so that priorities can be assigned to them.

Quality assurance, or "Q.A.," testers are the professionals who track down bugs and categorize them. Throughout the alpha and beta stages, Q.A. testers go through the title, clicking on every button, testing every feature, and keeping a record of every bug they find. They create a master list of fixes that are needed.

Testing is not limited to software alone. The process includes running the title on all of its anticipated "platforms" (Macintosh, Windows, etc.), because each computer has a different effect on a title's performance. Also, just before golden master stage, test CD-ROMs are pressed to ensure that the title runs properly as a CD-ROM.

This is the story of the Tortoise and the Hare.
Tortoise was a friendly fellow who moved
his own slow pace. The Hare was a busy
son who was always on the move.

Chevrolet

CALIFORNIA
WHAT YR?

FIELD
GUIDE

Garibaldi
(Hypsypops rubicundus)

Coordinates:
Depth: 15 ft.
Pressure: 2 Atm.
Temperature: 62°

Electric Blue?
The House Husband
Protected in California

Remarks: found ne
rocky sho
15 feet dee

THE ARCHITECTURE
OF MULTIMEDIA

Understanding the structural possibilities of multimedia is an often overlooked, yet necessary, step before you can effectively design a multimedia title. The following pages examine eight multimedia titles, each of which employs a unique structural model. From these examples you can begin to see how interactive multimedia structures accommodate a variety of information and cultivate many different kinds of user experiences.

The key to successful interactive stories is to create titles in which the environment is perhaps the most important "character."

—Ron Gilbert, Humongous Entertainment

HIERARCHY

One of the simplest ways to organize a multimedia title is through the use of a hierarchical system. This structure features a main menu screen that branches into other areas of the title. Depending upon the scope of the title, there may be multiple submenu screens branching users deeper and deeper into the title.

Perhaps the largest user interface problem with this structure is the ability to step back through the title—there is often more than one route to the same place. I have found that users frequently get lost in large titles that use a hierarchical structure.

Another drawback to this structure is that it gives few clues as to the scope of the title. People can follow a path without knowing how far it will go or what other areas are left to explore. When you pick up a book, you have an immediate sense of how large and complex it is just by its thickness. In a hierarchical multimedia structure, it's more difficult to tell how far you can or cannot go.

The flowchart diagram of the KidSoft CD-ROM on pages 12–13 maps out the architecture of a simple hierarchy.

FLATTENED HIERARCHY

A variation of a straight hierarchy is a flattened hierarchy. It is similar in structure in that users navigate from place to place through a sequence of branches. However, a flattened hierarchy features a series of "plateaus," or levels, in which multiple places are accessible from one screen. From each "flattened" plateau users can branch down into subplateaus.

Generally, navigation through this type of structure is accomplished by an ever-present set of icons, positioned in a consistent location on each screen (shown below), that represent each place on the plateau. These icons are buttons that quickly get a user around to the different places on a plateau until the user branches down a level by clicking somewhere in the content area. Peter Gabriel's *Xplora* title, developed by Brilliant Media, is an excellent example of this type of structure.

Overall, a flattened hierarchical structure is a good framework that allows users to "browse" a variety of media. Most authoring tools are capable of building hierarchical structures, but cards and stacks and time-based tools are particularly well suited for it (see Chapter 3, "A Look at Authoring Tools").

A series of icons representing all of the places on a particular plateau appear in a consistent location—the upper right—on each screen.

Xplora's main menu uses Peter Gabriel's face as a metaphor. Clicking on the eyes takes you to his "personal file," the nose brings you "behind the scenes," the mouth goes to the "US" section, and the ear sends you to the "world of music."

Clicking on Peter's eyes brings you to the first plateau. Notice that there are four places on this level—all represented by icons across the upper right that reflect imagery from each place. In the content area (below the icons), there are also four choices to branch you to a lower plateau.

Clicking on one of the buttons inside the content area brings you down a level into the next plateau.

How do you jump back up to a higher plateau? Xplora solved this problem by changing the normal arrow cursor temporarily into one of the above symbols when your mouse rolls into the upper area of the screen. Notice that these symbols reflect how many levels deep you are. Clicking when the cursor has become one of these symbols jumps you up to the first, second, or third level.

LINEAR

Another straightforward way to organize multimedia is with a linear structure in which media are presented more or less sequentially. While this kind of structure seems inherently opposed to what we think of as "interactive," the process of navigating back and forth and the inclusion of vignettes triggered by the user make linear structures just as interactive as other multimedia models.

Titles with a linear structure follow a predetermined course of action but offer localized interactions along the way. Users are able to trigger animated sequences, "flip" forward and back, or jump to any section of the title. This kind of structure lends itself well to storytelling and other linear information because it allows authors to retain control over the outcome and, to some degree, the presentation. One drawback to linear multimedia, however, is that users are more or less confined to a single experience—they're not allowed to explore content from other angles or to construct their own experience.

Living Books' *The Tortoise and the Hare* is an example of a linear narrative structure. This title is one in a series of children's stories complete with text and "pages" that users flip through. However, as the name implies, these "books" are brought to life with narration (available in multiple languages), music, and animation.

Linear structures can be created with most types of authoring tools. Living Books uses Macromedia Director, but they have modified it by developing custom extensions (see pages 42–43) that work well with their abundant animation and that enable them to reuse the software structure as a template for other titles in the series. Other tools recommended for linear structures are those based on the cards and stacks model.

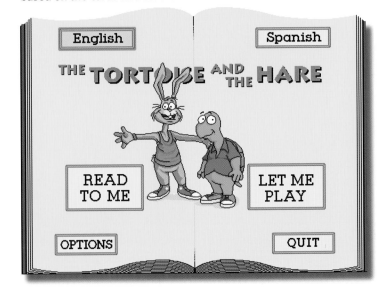

Simon, the host of Living Books' *The Tortoise and the Hare*, sets a warm tone in a short linear trailer introducing the story.

▲

Before you start the story, you can choose a language (English or Spanish) and whether or not you want the story read to you straight through on "autopilot"—without stopping to play.

1

This is the story of the Tortoise and the Hare. The Tortoise was a friendly fellow who moved at his own slow pace. The Hare was a busy person who was always on the move.

English

Everyone was excited on the day of the big race. The Hare was busy making sure everyone noticed him. The Tortoise could hardly believe that he was going to race.

OK ◄ 4 ►

Credits   Previews

From anywhere in the story, you can quickly jump to any page. A preview is offered for each page to help you decide where you want to go.

While the story is read aloud, the user is not able to interact with elements on the "page." After the page is read, the user is free to click on just about everything, triggering short animated segments that range from fun yet nonessential scenes to vignettes that enrich the story.

2

One day they ran into each other on the road. The Hare couldn't understand how the slow-moving Tortoise could accomplish anything.

The arrows on the bottom sides of the screen go to the next and previous pages. Also, notice how the portion of the text being read is highlighted.

3

The Tortoise and the Hare met again that afternoon. The Hare challenged the Tortoise to a race.

MULTITRACK

As its name suggests, a multitrack structure features multiple streams of synchronous media. This kind of structure is similar to a linear structure, but it goes one step further by including multiple overlapping linear structures. Think of yourself watching television, for example. There are many channels, each running one program, or "track." You choose to watch one show at a time, either by selecting one channel and staying with it or by using your remote control to "channel surf."

Unlike television, multitrack multimedia allows you to view a few programs—not necessarily all video-based—collaged together on the screen at one time. Users control which "tracks" of media they view or participate in as they roll forward through the title. The advantage over television is that users can go along at their own pace (go backward, pause, etc.) and content can be linked to additional in-depth information. For example, as you watch the full length of a movie you can click at any time in any scene to call up a sidebar, in an overlapping window, that has additional information specific to that scene. As you can see, this kind of structure could lend itself well to the future of television—interactive television.

David Rose of Interactive Factory has developed a multimedia version of *The Cartoon Guide to Physics*. This hands-on learning program lets you experiment with the laws of physics by placing such things as cars, balls, and springs onscreen so that you can test their velocity and other physical attributes. Ringo, a cartoon character, is your guinea pig—acting out experiments (such as being shot out of a cannon) with a touch of comic relief. Lucy, your host, acts as a guide.

There are two streams of information: "principles," in which Lucy provides in-depth information (such as equations and theorems) as your experiments take place, and "story," which prompts Lucy to explain in broader strokes the physics of your experiments. You can switch back and forth between the two tracks of information.

The Cartoon Guide to Physics is unique because it combines the multitrack structure with hands-on activities. Generally, multitrack and linear structures do not provide users with constructive experiences, such as model building or event simulation. Multitrack and linear structures are best used for presenting previously authored material (such as music, stories, movies, and reference information) that's enhanced by additional matter that can be called up by the user at will. Because the multitrack structure contains such linear, time-sensitive media, it's best supported by time-based authoring tools.

Interactive Factory's *The Cartoon Guide to Physics* is a hands-on, multitrack presentation of the laws of physics. Tools like the above stopwatch let you start and stop experiments. Lucy, your host (shown at right), guides you through the experiments.

A stack of rulers represents the two tracks of information. By clicking on a ruler, users choose which angle to view the material from—either the "story" of physics or the "principles" of physics.

MULTITRACK DIAGRAM

Multitrack structures feature multiple streams of synchronous media. (In this diagram, time rolls forward top to bottom.)

Track 1 — text
Track 2 — animation
Track 3 — video

Ringo, the cartoon character driving the car, carries out your experiments, while Lucy, the host, watches and explains what's going on.

Users control which combination of tracks they view or participate in as the presentation rolls forward.

INTERαCTIVE STⓞRIES

What does it mean to create a story in which the audience has control over its presentation—or even its outcome? Two structures featured on this page—a branching story structure and a web structure—address ways to organize such interactive stories for multimedia.

BRANCHING STORY STRUCTURE

A series of traditionally bound interactive books entitled *Choose Your Own Adventure*, developed by author R. A. Montgomery, was written to have many possible "endings." Each ending is the result of a unique set of decisions made throughout the story by the reader. For example, to use a tree metaphor, each reader starts at a common "trunk" and then branches out along different paths until he or she reaches a unique ending. This same kind of branching story structure can be applied to multimedia.

Greg Roach of HyperBole Studios has done innovative work in the area of branching multimedia stories. He's created titles in which users navigate through both video and 3-D virtual environments. The example shown on this page, *Quantum Gate*, features a

realistic environment in which the user "role-plays" a character through a variety of story possibilities.

Although branching stories are interesting ways to put the audience in control, they can be extremely costly and time-intensive to produce. You need to create a large repertoire of story possibilities in order to make each path into a single satisfactory story.

WEB STRUCTURE

Ron Gilbert, co-founder of Humongous Entertainment, developed a pioneering series of multimedia titles while at LucasGames, including *Maniac Mansion* and *The Secret of Monkey Island*, by using a unique cross between a branching story structure and traditional linear storytelling. I call it a "web" structure.

▲

This is one of the many linear pop-up scenes featured in HyperBole's *Quantum Gate*. Users are able to interrupt these scenes, but in doing so, they may miss out on valuable information.

Titles of this nature generally start out with a short linear sequence, or "cut scene," that sets the stage, introduces the characters, and provides information about the adventure that awaits you. Once the cut scene is over, you are left to explore a "web" of places where you can collect clues and meet more characters. At a certain point, such as when you solve a key puzzle, the title assumes you are ready for another cut scene to advance the story some more. The doors then open to a whole new environment, or web of places, you can explore. The story follows a predetermined course and has only one ending, but you are able to discover facets of the story in each web that opens up.

Interactive stories are more complex than the previous structures covered in this chapter. Time-based tools are capable of supporting this type of structure, but most likely you will need to develop custom extensions. Making the structure respond to all of the user's possible interactions and having the structure "know" when to initiate a cut scene are specialized features that require customization.

In Humongous Entertainment's *Freddi Fish and the Case of the Missing Kelp Seeds,* the user discovers the story as the result of exploring an interactive environment. After an initial cut scene introduces the main characters and the dilemma, the user is free to wander through the first "web" of places (shown below).

◄

The interface of *Quantum Gate* has multiple video windows overlapping a 3-D virtual environment. The user interacts with *Quantum Gate* by clicking either within the environment or on the icons peppered around the screen.

▶

After the user solves the first puzzle, the villains of *Freddi Fish* make their appearance in a cut scene—indicating that there is more going on in the story than meets the eye.

V⁶ᵢRTUAL SPₐCE

This is one of my favorite structures because I've seen it work in so many different ways, both literal and abstract. It consists of a familiar multidimensional space, such as a room or even a book, presented in such a way that users intuitively know how to navigate through it. For example, *Monterey Canyon's* "field guide" (shown on page 32) was designed to look like a book so that people could make quick assumptions about how to use it. Users can page back and forth, use the tabs to get to other sections, and close the guide when they are done—just as with a real book.

Using "virtual" everyday spaces and objects in multimedia leverages their natural "affordances," or clues (see Chapter 4, "User Interface Design"), to facilitate user interaction. For instance, people know through years of experience that a cutout in a wall filled with an object on hinges is a door . . . that leads somewhere else. Therefore, a door in a multimedia context naturally indicates to people that it will probably "take" them to a new place.

One drawback to emulating real-world spaces and objects, however, is that it can become tedious to the user to navigate in such a literal fashion. Let's say you are wandering through a virtual dollhouse. Going from one room to the next could involve navigating down a long series of hallways, wearing thin your

patience and stalling the flow of the experience. To solve this problem, you can abstract virtual spaces and objects so that they become metaphorical. To use the virtual dollhouse example again, when you want to navigate from room to room, a more abstract version of the interface might present a stylized version of the house, and you simply click on a representation of a room to instantly go there. This approach takes away the real-world constraints of getting from one place to the next, yet preserves the notion of a virtual house (after all, like movies, multimedia is not the real world, and people expect a little "magic" from it).

The virtual space example shown on this page is Presto Studios' *Buried in Time*. Users wander through a 3-D virtual environment as

This 3-D navigational tool in Presto Studios' *Buried in Time* accurately reflects the directions in which you can travel: forward, left and right, and up and down. Designers often have a difficult time translating movement through 3-D space onto a 2-D screen; for instance, sometimes a 2-D upward-pointing arrow is used to indicate forward 3-D movement.

© 1994 Presto Studios Inc.

seen through an electronic "eye patch." This artifice allows people to collect the information and tools they need throughout the game. Users can move forward, back, left, right, up, and down by using a 3-D navigational tool—underscoring the feeling that they are moving in a 3-D environment. When they move, the environment zooms in the appropriate direction as opposed to just cutting to the next scene. This simple detail helps to orient users and immerses them in the experience.

Intense, high-quality 3-D animation, which this title features, is notorious for slow performance. Therefore, Presto Studios decided to build Buried in Time in C, a low-level programming language (see pages 40–41), instead of using authoring tools such as Director or HyperCard. This allowed them to achieve faster "run-time" performance.

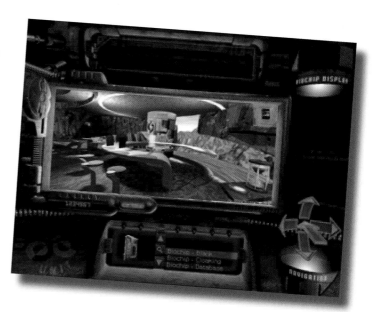

Buried in Time takes you on a journey to seven different time periods. Shown in these examples are scenes from medieval Europe (left), the future (right), and an ancient Mayan civilization (below).

A close-up of the environment from Buried in Time shows the intense realism and detail that can be achieved with 3-D modeling and rendering programs.

As you travel through time periods, you collect tools and "bio chips" that help you navigate through the game and solve the puzzle.

M⊙DULAR

Some multimedia titles are the result of multiple independent media objects coming together in different ways to create a custom experience for the user. Think of a line of children's toys like Barbie. All of the dolls, houses, clothing, and accessories are built to the same scale so that children can mix and match them to assemble a custom play experience. Pieces are independent of each other and thus can be sold separately or in pre-composed sets.

There are many advantages to this sort of modular design structure. First, users enjoy the flexibility of creating their own title based on their interests or needs. Second, titles of this nature can be continually expanded because new media objects can always be developed. This latter aspect is perhaps one of the most important

advantages because a lot of fixed titles suffer from low "replayability." Third, from a multimedia development point of view, a modular design can be a good investment. The creation of "mini multimedia objects" means a shorter development cycle, which, in turn, gets titles to market quickly.

One factor to consider, however, is that while media objects may be small in comparison to an entire title, ample time must be invested in the planning stages of a modular system. Although independent, all media objects of a series must follow a certain protocol so that they "know" how to bind together to create a single multimedia experience.

Kaleida's™ *Monterey Canyon* is a good example of a modular title. "Fish objects" are independent of the virtual Monterey Bay environment and thus can be used across a whole series of underwater exploration titles.

Object-oriented authoring tools (see pages 46–47) are best suited for creating modular titles because each object is treated individually and can be made either to stand alone from, or to integrate with, a variety of other objects.

Media objects, such as this octopus, are self-contained collections of animation and behaviors. Since they are independent of any greater structure, they can "plug and play" in any number of multimedia environments.

The field guide of Kaleida's *Monterey Canyon* is also an independent media object. It can be used to collect and identify fish across the whole series.

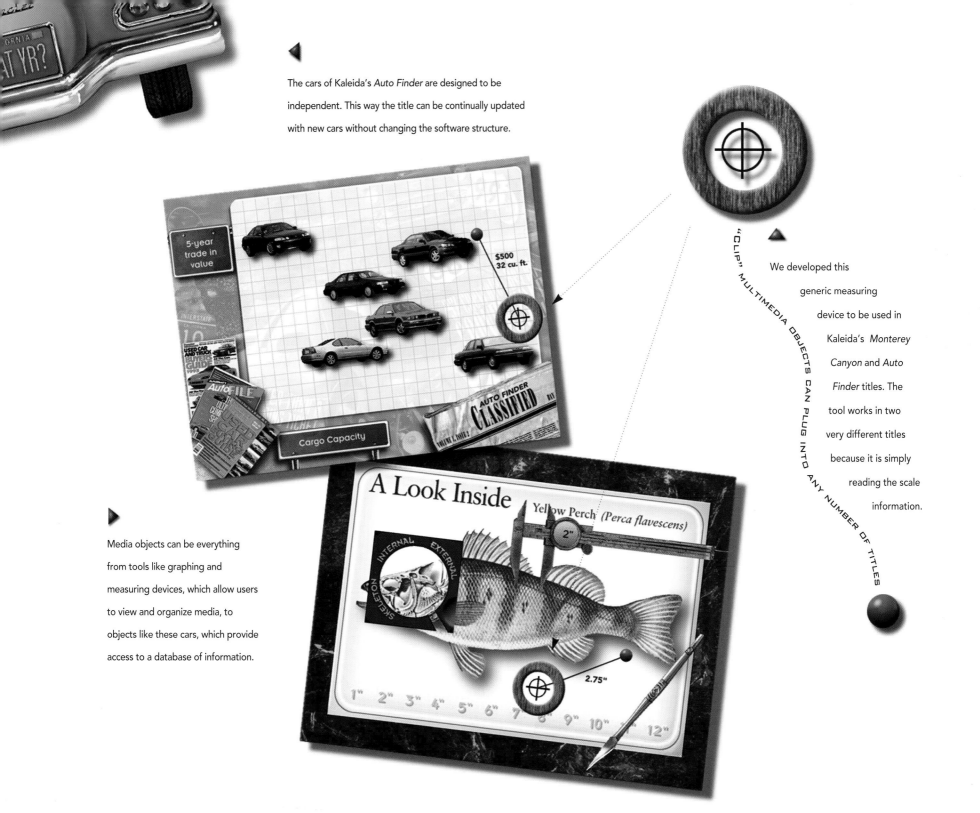

The cars of Kaleida's *Auto Finder* are designed to be independent. This way the title can be continually updated with new cars without changing the software structure.

We developed this generic measuring device to be used in Kaleida's *Monterey Canyon* and *Auto Finder* titles. The tool works in two very different titles because it is simply reading the scale information.

"CLIP" MULTIMEDIA OBJECTS CAN PLUG INTO ANY NUMBER OF TITLES

5-year trade in value

$500
32 cu. ft.

Cargo Capacity

AUTO FINDER CLASSIFIED

Media objects can be everything from tools like graphing and measuring devices, which allow users to view and organize media, to objects like these cars, which provide access to a database of information.

A Look Inside

Yellow Perch *(Perca flavescens)*

INTERNAL   EXTERNAL

SKELETON

2"

2.75"

1" 2" 3" 4" 5" 6" 7" 8" 9" 10" 11" 12"

C⦵NSTRUCTIVE

Like a modular structure, a constructive model features a collection of independent media objects. But in a constructive model, each object has a set of behaviors that have been engineered to create interesting and sometimes unpredictable interactions when two or more objects are juxtaposed. Much like the classic game *Mouse Trap*, in which a player builds a Rube Goldberg-like contraption to trap an unsuspecting mouse, half the fun of constructive titles is in assembling dynamic environments and seeing what happens.

The whole design paradigm of a constructive title is based on cause and effect. Therefore, when creating these kinds of titles, you need to think of all the possible uses and effects that each object can have—not just with one other object, but also in combination with multiple other objects. As you can imagine, the design process for a constructive title— working out all the interrelationships—can get fairly complicated.

Constructive structures work well for titles in which you would like to demonstrate cause and effect by virtue of putting two or more elements together. For instance, this structure would be ideal for a multimedia chemistry set. All the different substances could be combined and examined, allowing users the opportunity to experiment—safely—but still gain real-world results. As you can see, the constructive model is much like a simulation (see pages 36–37), but a constructive model is more limited in scope; it does not extend into modeling entire dynamic systems as they play out over time.

Authoring tools that support the creation of independent media objects are well suited for developing constructive titles. For instance, an object-oriented authoring tool (see pages 46–47) is a natural choice for creating constructive titles.

▲

In this constructive example I created, the cat's desire to pounce on the mouse is countered by his natural aversion to water. The clever mouse has harnessed the cat's nervous indecision to fuel a hot tub for himself.

Cables attached to the diving board oscillate up and down, driven by the cat's movement. The cables run through a pulley system down to an anvil suspended over a bellows. The anvil rises and falls over the bellows just enough to fuel the fire heating the water tank. The hot water then feeds into the mouse's hot tub.

One of my favorite examples of the constructive model is Sierra On-Line's *The Incredible Machine®*. This children's title offers a large inventory of fun everyday objects that can be assembled in countless ways to create a seemingly endless array of little machines, from conveyor belts to gear systems.

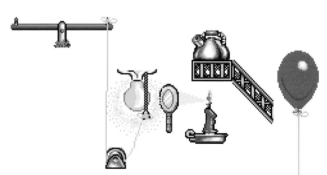

S⁶₁MULATION

Multimedia is an excellent medium for emulating real-life systems. For example, look at the popular simulation series developed by Maxis—*SimLife*, *SimCity*, *SimEarth*, and others—that put users in control of life-forms, towns, and worlds. *SimEarth*, for instance, equips you with a palette of life "building blocks," a blank planet, and a couple of environmental and weather controls that you can manipulate in order to create a thriving planet.

In a multimedia simulation, individual objects, such as animals, factories, etc., have been designed with a set of "behaviors" that respond to conditions set by the user. For instance, if the user brought out some "food" objects, the hungry "animal" objects may stop what they are doing and come to eat. This action might trigger another chain of events and so on and so on. Once set in motion, the simulated environment evolves over time and is modeled on a real-life situation.

The growth speed-o-meter of C-Wave's *Forever Growing Garden* lets the user control the passage of time and thus, the growth rate of the gardens.

In *Forever Growing Garden*, created by C-Wave, you are presented with three garden settings: a home garden, a vegetable patch, and castle grounds. After choosing one, you make a quick visit to the hardware shop where you select seeds that are appropriate for that type of garden. You can plant your seeds, and with the help of some gardening tools, such as a watering can, a shovel, and a pair of gloves, you can begin to grow your garden.

Simulation environments are best supported by object-oriented authoring tools. If your simulation is very complex, however, you may need to custom-build the title in a low-level programming language.

An overhead view of the countryside is the main menu. From here, you choose a place to start: the castle grounds, the home garden, or the country vegetable patch. You can have gardens growing simultaneously in all three places.

This simulation also has a degree of modularity. The seed packets were engineered to stand alone from the title. In addition to the built-in set, other seed packets may be purchased separately so that you can continually customize your garden.

TOM-A-TOES

FLOWER

MONSTER SQUASH

TULIP

PUMPKIN

SKYVIEW

TOOLS LIKE THIS WATERING CAN HELP PROVIDE A REALISTIC FEEL TO THE SIMULATION

```
LxMemHandle far __pascal __export _KIDSOFT_mGetWorkingDir (
    LxProcTablePtr  xtbl,
    LxMemHandle  hKidsoft)

LxMemHandle hStrMsg;
P_KIDSOFT_DATA pKidsoft;

pKidsoft = xtbl->mem_Lock(hKidsoft);

hStrMsg = xtbl->string_New(pKidsoft->hardDrive);
xtbl->mem_Unlock(hKidsoft);

return hStrMsg;
```

CHAPTER 3

A LOOK AT
AUTHORING TOOLS

This chapter examines the different kinds of authoring tools people use to create multimedia titles. Authoring tools are software packages that you can buy from your local computer store. Just as Photoshop is designed for preparing graphics, authoring tools are designed to "wire" media together once they have been prepared. Since there are so many tools to choose from, and new ones are always being introduced, I have organized this chapter into four categories of authoring tools: low-level programming languages, time-based tools, "cards and stacks," and object-oriented tools.

Just as architects must understand the properties of steel, concrete, and wood—even though they may never set a brick—multimedia designers must understand the nature of the tools and materials from which multimedia experiences are built.

—Steve Gano, Modular Arts

FR⊙M THE GR⊙UND UP

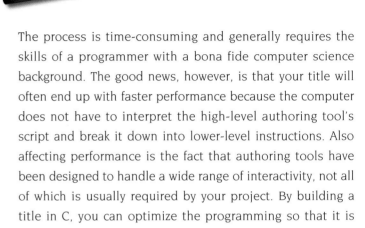

Highly detailed 3-D animated scenes such as these from Presto Studios' *The Journeyman Project Turbo* create drag on the computer system because colors and textures are changing all over the scene at once. The computer has to constantly "redraw" the whole scene, not just localized areas.

"Low-level" programming languages such as C and C++ are the building blocks for most consumer software. As bricks are to buildings, low-level languages are the foundation of "high-level" software applications (see sidebar at right), from word processing programs to multimedia authoring tools. And just as these low-level languages can be used to build authoring tools like Director (see pages 42–43), they can also be used to build multimedia titles—from the ground up.

BEST USES

Because there are so many powerful high-level authoring tools available, it is not often that a multimedia title needs to be created entirely from scratch using a low-level language. There are times, however, when high-level tools have their limitations. Although they are easy to use and are able to quickly assemble media into multimedia titles, high-level tools often can't handle fancy interactive animation sequences, complex simulations, or intricate constructive environments.

In these cases, you must create the title by using one of the low-level languages.

The process is time-consuming and generally requires the skills of a programmer with a bona fide computer science background. The good news, however, is that your title will often end up with faster performance because the computer does not have to interpret the high-level authoring tool's script and break it down into lower-level instructions. Also affecting performance is the fact that authoring tools have been designed to handle a wide range of interactivity, not all of which is usually required by your project. By building a title in C, you can optimize the programming so that it is more specific to your title's needs.

The intense 3-D animation of Presto Studios' *The Journeyman Project Turbo*, for example, performed slowly on Windows machines. Therefore, the decision was made to invest time and money in building the Windows version in C in order to boost performance.

The amount of screen space used in multimedia titles for video and animation is limited because of performance issues. Currently, a large video or animation window significantly slows the playback or causes scenes to be dropped out altogether.

Throughout this chapter I include small samples of programming to give you an idea of what it looks like for each type of authoring tool. The example at right is an X object (written in C code) from the KidSoft CD-ROM.

```
#include <windows.h>
#include "XObject.h"

typedef struct
{
    LxXObjHeader        head;        // Required XObject header

    char                hardDrive[256]; // the directory
} KIDSOFT_DATA, FAR *P_KIDSOFT_DATA;

LxMemHandle __far __pascal __export _KIDSOFT_mGetWorkingDir (
    LxProcTablePtr  xtbl,
    LxMemHandle  hKidsoft)
{
    LxMemHandle hStrMsg;
    P_KIDSOFT_DATA pKidsoft;

    pKidsoft = xtbl->mem_Lock(hKidsoft);

    hStrMsg = xtbl->string_New(pKidsoft->hardDrive);
    xtbl->mem_Unlock(hKidsoft);

    return hStrMsg;
}
```

Continuum

Authoring tools and programming languages can be placed on a continuum of "user friendliness" extending from raw binary machine language at the bottom on up to what looks like written English at the top.

High-level authoring tools	Director Authorware HyperCard Apple Media Tool mTropolis
Mid-level scripting languages	HyperTalk Lingo
	ScriptX
Low-level programming languages	C++ C
Lowest-level programming languages	Assembly Language
	Machine Language

```
on toggleAnim
  --beep()
  set jeff= the clickOn
  put the clickon
  If the clickon =14 then
    set kRecordSpr = 2
  else if the clickOn = 15 then
    set KRecordSpr = 12
  end if

  set the constraint of sprite KRecordSpr=kConstrainSpr
  If the clickon = 14 then
    set gCurSequence=value (line 1 of field "sequence data")
  else if the clickon = 15 then
    set gCurSequence=value (line 1 of field "Anim 2 sequence")
  end if

end ToggleAnim

on toggleTrack
  if the clickon = 16 then
    set track = 1
  else if the clickon = 17 then
    set track = 2
  end if
end toggle Track
```

T̈I̊ME-BASED

One of the most popular "off-the-shelf" multimedia authoring tools today is Macromedia Director. Store-bought authoring tools have a relatively easy-to-use "graphical user interface," or GUI (pronounced "goo-ey"), that allows people without a computer science background to create multimedia applications. Notice that Director is referred to as a tool and not a language. Tools like Director are software applications that have been built from low-level programming languages (see pages 40–41).

Director is a "time-based" authoring tool. Just as a sequence of still frames comprises a filmstrip, Director works by composing a multimedia title one "frame," or scene, at a time. The metaphor Director uses to do this is a movie or theater set—hence the name Director. You are the director manipulating media on the stage and assigning them instructions by writing "script" in a special window called the "Score" (shown at right). Media are stored in a special collection window called the "Cast" (shown below). Director's stage metaphor implies that various media are like actors, props, and backdrops.

Scenes are composed by selecting various "cast members" and placing them on the main screen, or "stage."

SCRIPTING LANGUAGES

Most authoring tools come equipped with their own "scripting" language—a "mid-level" programming language (see sidebar on page 41) that allows you to build fairly complex multimedia structures. Director's scripting language, "Lingo," is quite robust—it's able to accomplish most of the specialized tasks you can dream up. Scripting is programming, but the "code" you write in Director looks and reads a lot like English; for example, "go to frame 5" is a simple Lingo script.

Macromedia Director stores media in the "Cast" window. Each cell of the Cast window shows a thumbnail representation of the media it contains.

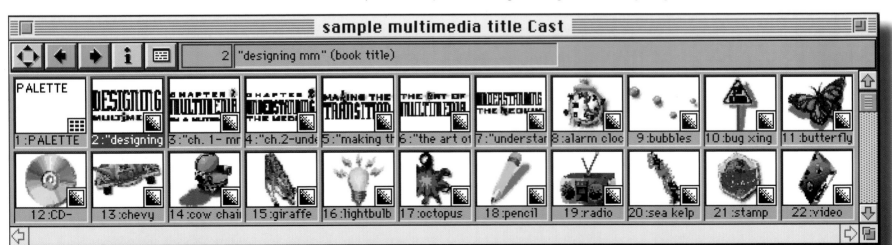

sample multimedia title Cast

2 | "designing mm" (book title)

| 1 :PALETTE | 2 :"designing | 3 :"ch. 1- mn | 4 :"ch.2-und | 5 :"making th | 6 :"the art o | 7 :"understar | 8 :alarm cloc | 9 :bubbles | 10 :bug xing | 11 :butterfly |
| 12 :CD- | 13 :chevy | 14 :cow chai | 15 :giraffe | 16 :lightbulb | 17 :octopus | 18 :pencil | 19 :radio | 20 :sea kelp | 21 :stamp | 22 :video |

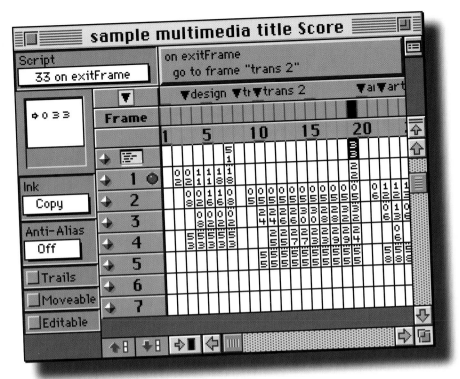

A separate window called the "Score" provides a visual log of each frame, showing both the media and the scripts it contains (notice the longer sample of Lingo script at left). In addition, Director offers built-in transitions, such as dissolves, and ink effects, such as key color transparency (see Chapter 5, "Graphic Production Tips and Strategies"), all of which are accessible from the Score.

Because Living Books titles have so many animated scenes and characters, Director was a natural choice as their basic authoring environment. An object-oriented tool could build each title, but synchronizing the animation of multiple objects is not worth the effort when compared to Director's natural ability. A cards and stacks tool is not a good choice either, because flipping through a series of cards or writing extensions to display so much animation is inefficient.

For the times that even the mid-level scripting language falls short, Director and many other authoring tools allow you to extend their scripting language with "X objects" or "X commands" (segments of C code) to get the job done.

BEST USES

As you can see, the popularity of these high-level tools can be attributed to both their versatility as tools and their flexibility in integrating with low-level languages. Time-based tools are good for creating multitrack, linear, and hierarchical structures—especially those with a lot of animation. Time-based tools are also good for creating simple interactive story structures, but most likely you will need to develop custom extensions for more complicated story structures. As mentioned on page 40, one drawback is that complex multimedia titles authored with high-level tools tend to perform much slower.

CaRDS & STaCKS

For all intents and purposes, the first multimedia "titles," as we know them, used an authoring tool called HyperCard, introduced by Apple in 1987. HyperCard uses the metaphor of index cards, and stacks of index cards, to organize media. A card may contain a variety of media elements, including buttons that link to other cards. A group of cards interlinked together in a coherent structure becomes a stack. Stacks, in turn, can be linked to other stacks, and so on and so on.

▲

One of the first "titles" to be authored in HyperCard was a MacWorld Expo kiosk, created by Kristee Rosendahl at the Apple Multimedia Lab in 1987. The first versions of HyperCard supported only one-bit graphics—limiting the palette to black and white.

MYST

Shown at right is Cyan's *Myst*, one of the more complex titles that has been authored in HyperCard. *Myst* is a tricky one because it features a 3-D virtual world that you can explore. If you look closely, however, you notice that you move through it one frame at a time, or one card at a time. There are small localized animations in each scene, but for the most part you move through static scenes (cards) that have buttons (links). The creators of *Myst* wrote a lot of custom code extensions (X commands) in order to accomplish everything they wanted—especially the animation. But the underlying tool for this beautiful and complex title is plain old HyperCard.

BEST USES

At first thought, a cards and stacks type of authoring tool seems to be well suited for modular title design. Notice, however, that cards and stacks are interlinked, thus relatively interdependent. The modular structure (discussed on pages 32–33) calls for each of the multimedia objects to be independent of each other and able to bind together in different combinations. Cards and stacks establish rigid connections that do not allow for such mixing and matching.

The concept of cards and stacks is a fairly straightforward organizing principle. It works well for titles featuring

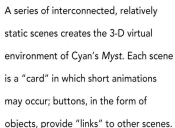

A series of interconnected, relatively static scenes creates the 3-D virtual environment of Cyan's *Myst*. Each scene is a "card" in which short animations may occur; buttons, in the form of objects, provide "links" to other scenes.

interconnected pagelike structures, like reference titles, but not so well for titles featuring dynamic, heavily animated environments, such as *The Journeyman Project*. Hierarchies, linear narratives, interactive stories with limited animation (such as *Myst*), and simple constructive and simulation titles are structures readily created with a cards and stacks authoring tool such as HyperCard.

Users navigate from scene to scene (card to card) in *Myst* by moving the cursor to the edges of the screen. The cursor changes into a pointing hand indicating the direction of travel: forward, backward, left, and right. Users click to travel in the desired direction. Also, users may click on objects they encounter, such as the switch in this scene.

```
on open Stack
  if wrongStack() then pass openStack
  create TheMenu
  pass openStack
end openStack


on closeStack
  if wrongStack() then pass closeStack
  global ErrandsFind
  deleteStackMenu
  put empty into ErrandsFind
  pass closeStack
end closeStack


on openBackground
  changeMenuItemStatus
  setLocationCheckMark
  pass openBackground
end openBackground
```

This is a small sample of HyperCard's scripting language, called HyperTalk. As you can see, HyperTalk is very similar to Lingo (shown on page 42).

CRoSS-PLATFoRM

When a title is "cross-platform," it means that one version of the title is able to play back on more than one type of computer. Rarely, however, are titles built just once that are then able to play back on multiple platforms. Since each type of computer has a unique underlying software architecture, a title generally needs to be reengineered in order to conform to each standard!

As daunting a task as that may seem, there are some high-level tools, like Director, that have two versions—one for Macintosh and one for Windows—that work together to ease cross-platform development. Once a title is created on one platform, it may be saved in such a way that it works on another platform.

Most high-level authoring tools, however, have been designed to take advantage of a particular platform—either Mac or Windows. Therefore, titles created with these tools will also be platform-specific.

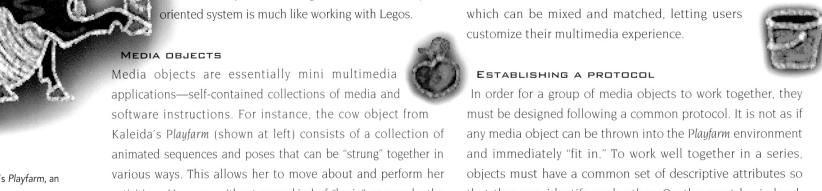

OBJeCT-ORiENTED

Authoring tools like mTropolis, Apple Media Tool and Kaleida's ScriptX™ merge object-oriented software technology with multimedia. The basic unit in any multimedia object-oriented system is the individual media object. Because everything revolves around individual objects, building a title with an object-oriented system is much like working with Legos.

MEDIA OBJECTS

Media objects are essentially mini multimedia applications—self-contained collections of media and software instructions. For instance, the cow object from Kaleida's *Playfarm* (shown at left) consists of a collection of animated sequences and poses that can be "strung" together in various ways. This allows her to move about and perform her activities. However, without some kind of "brain" or agenda, the cow—as an independent object—would have no way of assembling and presenting herself. Therefore, she has been endowed with a "character engine"—a system that takes into account her surrounding environment, her mood, and her personality and then calls up the appropriate sounds and animations in response to stimuli.

DYNAMIC BINDING

Object-oriented authoring tools feature "dynamic binding"—the ability to allow individual objects to bind together while the title is running. *Playfarm* consists of three different kinds of objects: characters like the cow, props such as apples and buckets, and fixtures like the barn and fences—all of which can be mixed and matched, letting users customize their multimedia experience.

ESTABLISHING A PROTOCOL

In order for a group of media objects to work together, they must be designed following a common protocol. It is not as if any media object can be thrown into the *Playfarm* environment and immediately "fit in." To work well together in a series, objects must have a common set of descriptive attributes so that they can identify each other. On the most basic level, *Playfarm* objects identify each other as either characters, props, or fixtures. Each type of object then has a standard group of categories set up for further identification (in the case of a prop like an apple, these might include categories like "edible?"—yes, "type of food?"—veggie, etc.). Therefore, when designing a series of objects, you need to think about how to categorize them.

For Kaleida's *Playfarm*, an object-oriented authoring tool was needed in order to create autonomous characters that could be added to or subtracted from the title now and in the future. *Playfarm*, authored in ScriptX, was inspired by *Playmobil*, a modular line of children's toys.

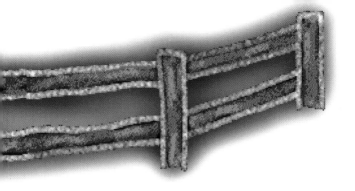

◀

The goose's "character engine" is sensitive to a disorderly environment. When things are out of place, the goose becomes agitated and starts ordering the other characters around.

By establishing a common protocol, new media objects may be developed and introduced at a later date and still integrate with the rest of the series. The advantage to this is that an entire ongoing line of multimedia products may be developed.

CROSS-PLATFORM DEVELOPMENT

Many object-oriented tools allow cross-platform development. ScriptX is low-level enough that you can develop the title once (for the most part) and then play it back on both Windows and Macintosh platforms. Apple Media Tool provides a way to save either a Windows or a Mac version when you are done scripting. Even though these tools allow for cross-platform authoring, they cannot guarantee trouble-free porting from one platform to the other—some additional handwork is almost always needed.

BEST USES

Object-oriented authoring tools are capable of building all the structures outlined in Chapter 2; they're especially good at creating modular structures. Titles that rely heavily on animation, however, are probably better off using a time-based tool.

This is an early example of ScriptX code used to add the barn fixture to the *Playfarm* landscape.

```
-- Method addBarn adds the barn object to the playfarm environment.
method addBarn self {class PlayfarmManager} #key media: sound: ->
(
 local barn := new BarnPresenter media:media sound:sound
 barn.z := 1
 local modelProp := new PropShell propPresent:barn

 addToScene modelProp theModelGrid theSceneSpace
 modelprop.shelltype := @prop
 barn.x := 45

 modelProp.attributes := new SortedKeyedArray \
  initialSize: 3 \
  keys: #(@category, @size, @moveable) \
  values: #(@item, @extralarge, @false)
 )
```

Catherine,
I've left for you a message of utmost importance in our fore-chamber beside the dock. Enter the number of Marker Switches on this island into the imager to retrieve the message.
Yours,
Atrus

I|O

button

button

RESTART
HELP
INFO
SCORES
GAMES
STUDIO
EXIT

KIDSOFT SUPER STORE
THE KIDSOFT
CLUB ROOM
CLUB ART
Club TV
CLUB Story
CONTEST CENTRAL
PIZZA PI PIZZA PI
SPELL'N
DEMOS

TRAVELRAMA USA
NEW GAME
EXIT   TOUR   ALBUM

LIST OF PLAYERS
● Kathy
  Blinky
  Big Mamma
  The Duke
  Mike
  T.J.

TRAVELRAMA
ISSUED TO
Kathy
DRIVING RECORD
GAMES PLAYED O
GAMES WON   O
☒ LEARNER'S PERMIT
☐ DRIVER'S LICENSE
OFFICIAL LEARNER'S P

CHAPTER 4

USER INTERFACE
DESIGN

A collection of media is formless and meaningless if there is no means to navigate through it or experience it. User interface design is the process of ergonomically and strategically presenting media in order to communicate a message. Whether the message is informational, emotional, or navigational, there are a number of user interface conventions that are your tools for communicating through multimedia.

Interface design isn't about icons and buttons any more than graphic design is about typefaces and bleeds. They are both about creating experiences and communicating emotions and information.

—Nathan Shedroff, vivid studios

DeSIGNING AN INTeRFACE

The "tabletop-like" interface from the 1987 MacWorld Expo kiosk, designed by Kristee Rosendahl, was meant to resemble a typical collection of information you pick up on the way into a convention. The tabletop metaphor provided a familiar, graphical way to display the choices to the user. This pioneering piece demonstrates interface design principles that still hold true today.

▼

User interface design is not just about the arrangement and presentation of media on the screen, it's about designing an entire experience for people. It involves psychological aspects, such as building a mental picture in a user's mind of how something works, and ergonomic issues, such as navigation and ways in which multimedia responds to a user's actions.

Because of its integral importance, user interface is the driving force behind both the structural and the graphic design decisions of a multimedia title. One of the largest misconceptions people have is that user interface is something that can be thrown on at the end like wallpaper. User interface design, however, provides a structure and an environment that best communicates content.

VISUAL DESIGNERS TAKING THE LEAD

With the arrival of "graphical user interfaces" (GUIs, pronounced "goo-eys") in the software industry, the first "user interface designers" were culled more from the academic ranks of clinical psychology than from visual design fields. This tradition carried over into multimedia—carving out user

interface design as a separate profession from that of graphic design. The principles of interface design, however, are drawn from basic communication design and industrial design. Therefore, graphic designers and industrial designers find user interface design a natural extension of their traditional training. Today the crossover is more apparent as visual designers are designing not only the graphic "look" but also the interactive structure and "feel" of multimedia.

THREE STEPS TO DESIGNING A USER INTERFACE

How do you go about designing an interface that is not only functional but experiential? Below are three steps to help you start designing an interface.

1) IDENTIFY YOUR AUDIENCE AND MESSAGE

The first step is to determine who your audience is and what you are trying to say to them. How old is your primary audience? What kind of experience and structure do you think they will respond to? Are they people who will understand a subtle interface and be eager to explore it? Are they people who are not yet comfortable with multimedia and need a hand-holding interface? Many fancy interfaces only work well for a limited, more experienced audience.

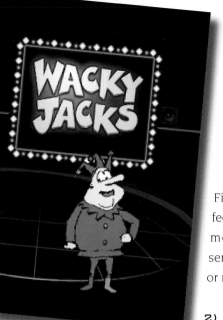

Zenda Studio's *Wacky Jacks* is an educational "game show" that features a variety of puzzles and trivia games. Players pick contestants from the studio audience, select a level of difficulty, and then choose a game.

Finally, decide on the look and feel that would best convey your message—is it sinister or serious, rich in color and texture or minimalist?

2) DETERMINE THE SETTING

An often overlooked aspect of user interface design is the setting in which people use multimedia. Designers need to know how and where users will be interacting with a multimedia title. Is it at home or in the office, in a museum or other public space, with a desktop PC or a handheld computer, or at home sitting on the couch interacting with the television? Is it a personal one-on-one experience or will many people be gathered around? Lastly, how much time will people spend with the title? Multimedia made for public spaces, for example, requires the designer to create a simplified interface that quickly delivers the message.

3) CREATE AN EXPERIENCE

Another decision you need to make is about the kind of experience you want users to have. Do you want them to go on a journey or to just have fun exploring? Do you want them to feel as if they are taking on a role or as if they are part of a conversation? *Wacky Jacks*, an educational title for kids developed by Zenda Studio, creates the experience of being a contestant on a game show. Another approach to delivering multimedia educational material might be to use a book metaphor, as in Dorling Kindersley's *My First, Incredible, Amazing Dictionary* (shown at right).

The "album" section of *Wacky Jacks* (shown at left) provides a visual reference of the people, animals, places, and things used in the games. Above is a "page" from Dorling Kindersley's *My First, Incredible, Amazing Dictionary*. Compare the two very different ways of delivering similar information: One adopts a game show format, while the other uses a book metaphor.

FoRM & FUNCTIoN

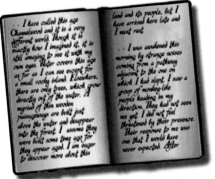

The background story of *Myst* is available in books found in the library, one of the central buildings on the island.

A scene from Cyan's *Myst*—one of the best-selling CD-ROMs to date. Part of the reason this game is so popular is its interface. The entire screen is filled with the content of the game. There are no buttons, icons, or menu bars to detract from the experience.

Once you have identified your audience, determined the setting, and decided upon the experience you would like to create, it is time to figure out how to implement the title in terms of actual functionality. For instance, how would you support a game show experience like the one in *Wacky Jacks*? How do players know whose turn it is? How do they initiate game play? The following guidelines are helpful when thinking about questions of functionality.

LESS IS MORE

Determine how much functionality users really need—especially at one time. Since multimedia has limited screen real estate, more options only clutter the screen, confuse the user, and detract from the experience.

CONSISTENCY

Decide on the functions that users should always be able to access wherever they are in the title. Whatever those functions are (to quit, to restart, or to go back), they should be located in

the same place and be graphically represented in the same way throughout the title. Methods of interaction should also remain consistent. For instance, if audio clues are used to indicate which areas are "active," then there should be no active areas without an audio track. Consistency builds confidence in the user. Once users trust that certain options will always be available, they will feel free to explore further.

THREE STEPS AWAY

Do not bury functions and places so deep in a title that they are more than three clicks away from any one location. Hierarchical structures, for instance, are notorious for having too many steps to reach the desired result. In fact, flattened hierarchies were invented as a way to limit the amount of navigational steps between the different areas of a title.

TRANSPARENCY

Good interface design, it is argued, can be judged by the degree that it goes unnoticed. If people spend all their time just figuring it out, they become focused away from the actual content of the title. The most transparent interfaces are those in which all functionality is embedded in the content. The interface functions of *Myst*,

Clicking on Wacky, the host of Zenda Studio's *Wacky Jacks*, causes him to reach in and uncurl a list of common controls. This way, these items are always available yet can be neatly tucked away.

for example, are extremely transparent. Users are completely immersed in the content—the content is the interface. *Myst* features no visible "buttons" per se or even a collection of icons; instead it relies entirely on the environment as a means of interaction. The cursor (onscreen pointer) is a hand image that changes according to what you can do as you move it around different areas of the screen. If you move off to the left of the screen, the hand points left, indicating that you could walk left (if you clicked). In another example, background information about the story is found in books in the library (shown above left).

ANTICIPATION

Like the changing hand cursor of *Myst*, functions within a title are usually context-sensitive—meaning that they are only relevant at certain times and in certain places. Therefore, it does not make sense to have all of the functions available at one time. Multimedia that anticipates a user's actions and provides the appropriate functions at the right time creates a more dynamic experience and supports the "less is more" philosophy.

Users interact with *Myst* by moving the cursor around the environment. The cursor changes according to what you can do: move around or activate items in the environment.

BaRS, PANeLS, & DRAWeRS

A common way to handle functionality in a title is to group functions in a special location such as a navigation bar, a control panel, or a drawer. Grouping functions by location clarifies an interface.

NAVIGATION BARS

Satisfying the need for consistency in a user interface, "navigation bars" provide a dedicated space for navigational functions such as quitting, going back, and moving from place to place. Such a neat, contained space orients users in a title. Like a dashboard on a car, however, a navigation bar tends to look mechanical. In terms of visual design, this can be problematic if the rest of the title "feels" organic. As a designer, you must think of ways to integrate the navigational controls so that they blend into the style of the title.

CONTROL PANELS

Like navigation bars, control panels provide a dedicated space for global functions (functions the user has access to at all times). They are essentially the same as navigation bars, but control panels are not necessarily limited to navigational functions.

DRAWERS

Not only do control panels and navigational bars tend to be mechanical, but they also take up valuable screen space. Therefore, you may want to consider a collapsed, "closed" state for them, called a drawer (shown above left).

Ergonomics

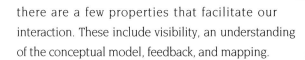

Each issue of the KidSoft CD features a thematic "Clubroom" activity space just for kids. The consistent use of a room metaphor helps keep users oriented from issue to issue.

▼

THE ERGONOMICS OF EVERYDAY THINGS

In our everyday lives we are surrounded by tools and machines that we interact with. Think of your car, for example. The arrangement of features has been carefully thought out for decades now—even the choice of features. The important, frequently used functions are up front on the dashboard, while the less-used features are housed elsewhere or even under the hood. How do we "know" how to use everyday things? As Donald Norman has identified in his book, *The Psychology of Everyday Things,*

there are a few properties that facilitate our interaction. These include visibility, an understanding of the conceptual model, feedback, and mapping.

VISIBILITY

Visuals play a key role in user interface design because people rely heavily on eyesight to interact with the world. On the multimedia screen, it is the visual design that first entices us to interact with media, then gives us clues about how to interact. One large misconception is that designers can come in at the end of a project to simply "make it look nice." On the contrary, visuals are an essential part of interface design.

CONCEPTUAL MODEL

Metaphorical models help people navigate through multimedia by giving them a strong "sense of place." Having an overall mental picture of how something works or how something is put together gives people a better understanding of its interface—even when they are viewing only a small portion at a time. When you are looking at a street map for example, the conceptual model is that of an aerial view of a vast expanse. Though you're looking at only a small section at any one time, your mind's eye knows that there are adjacent areas accessible by simply panning around the map.

From time to time, a mailbox pops up with new e-mail for the kids. Not only does the use of a real-life mailbox identify the new messages as mail, but there is also no question about what the user has to do to get the mail—the metaphorical model of the mailbox as a container is well known.

FEEDBACK

When people interact with machines, they expect some form of acknowledgment to help them determine that what they are doing is correct or that everything is in proper working order. For instance, turning the key to start a car should produce a healthy "vroooom" of the engine. The same concept applies to designing an interface for multimedia. For instance, when people click on a "hot spot" (see sidebar at right) to initiate an action, they want immediate reassurance that the system did in fact receive their command. All media, including animation and sound, become instrumental in providing feedback. Sometimes a short audio segment is enough to assure users that the computer is responding to them.

MAPPING

Designers need to present interface functions in such a way that the user's expectations of what will happen match the actual results when clicked. For instance, if you clicked on the above mailbox, you would expect the drawer to open, revealing mail inside. If it "mooed" and nothing else happened, you would be caught off-guard and think, "Why is this a mailbox?" The coordination of expectations and results is not an easy task, especially when using abstract metaphors. How many times have you seen a question mark icon and known exactly what you would get if you clicked it? Does it mean help or more info? The best way to find out how well your interface functions map to people's expectations is to conduct user tests.

The button in the Clubroom that takes you to the software demos is a "three-state button." There is a normal resting state (top), a roll-over state (middle), and a clicked state (bottom). Such feedback is consistent throughout the KidSoft CD.

HOT SPOTS

Hot spots are the areas on the screen that are currently interactive. How does the user distinguish these so-called hot spots from the rest of the screen? Part of the user interface design problem is to think of ways to identify these areas by using not only metaphorical visual clues (see pages 56–57), but also audio and animated feedback.

FEEDBACK

An important part of multimedia user interface design, feedback not only lets users know whether or not the computer is responding, but it also may help to guide the flow of user interaction. For instance, if certain sounds are produced or certain objects become animated while users are simply moving the cursor aimlessly around the screen, the users may be inclined to explore those areas further.

ROLL-OVER AND HIGHLIGHT STATES

To help identify hot spots, a common user interface design practice is to provide animated "roll-over" states. These are altered graphics that display themselves when the user simply "rolls" over a hot spot with the cursor. For example, while the user is just moving the cursor around the screen looking for things to do, certain graphics will change or highlight as the cursor passes over them. This way, users can easily get a sense of what's clickable.

METAPHORS & AFFORDANCES

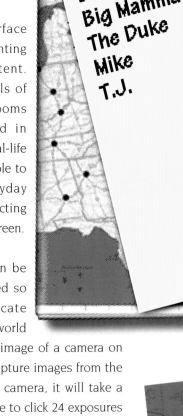

LIST OF PLAYERS

●Kathy
Blinky
Big Mamma
The Duke
Mike
T.J.

Travelrama, developed by Zenda Studio, is a "road trip" adventure across America. Notice that on the introductory screen, the way to start the game is by clicking on the key. Such use of metaphors not only helps users navigate the title but also is an opportunity to play off the game's theme.

▼

The most obvious elements of a user interface are its visuals. But because the screen is filled with visuals of all kinds, how do users distinguish the hot spots from the rest of the screen? Moreover, how do they know what to do with those items? Should they click on them, click and drag them, or what? Part of the user interface design problem is to think of ways to identify these areas by using not only metaphorical visual clues, but also audio clues.

TRAVELRAMA DMV

ISSUED TO
Kathy

DRIVING RECORD
GAMES PLAYED 0
GAMES WON 0
☒ LEARNER'S PERMIT
☐ DRIVER'S LICENSE

OFFICIAL LEARNER'S PERMIT

DIRECTOR OF LICENSES & PERMITS

one of the most popular interface conventions for organizing and presenting multimedia content. Metaphorical models of maps, books, and rooms are frequently used in multimedia titles. Real-life metaphors allow people to apply their everyday experiences to interacting with content on the screen.

METAPHORS

Because interacting with a computer can be an abstract way of getting information, it helps to use familiar conceptual models to orient users. For instance, both Macintosh and Windows computers use the notion of a "desktop," complete with drawers and folders, to organize the whole system. (Compare this way of interacting with computers to the "command line" approach of twelve years ago.)

Using real-life objects and situations as models has become

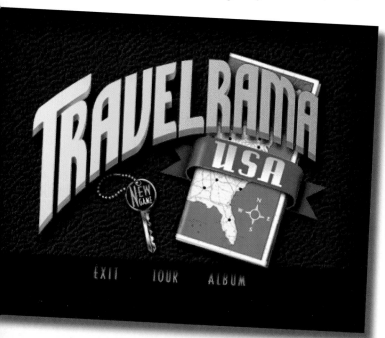

TRAVELRAMA USA

NEW GAME

EXIT   TOUR   ALBUM

Real-world metaphors, however, can be taken too far. Metaphors implemented so literally that they exactly duplicate interactions as they occur in the real world become a nuisance. For instance, the image of a camera on the screen suggests to me that I can capture images from the title. I assume that by clicking on the camera, it will take a picture and store it somewhere. If I have to click 24 exposures and then press a separate "develop film" button, forget it!

AFFORDANCES

While metaphors reveal a title's conceptual model of interaction, affordances are the little details that tell us specifically what the images are and how we should use

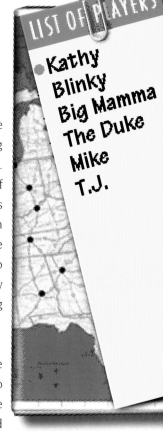

Before you start the game, you must choose either a preset or a stored player name, or enter a new name on the driver's license (shown below left).

them. There is a certain literacy associated with the operation of everyday things. For instance, just by seeing a doorknob, people know that they must twist then push or pull it to open the door. But on a computer screen, people must first recognize the graphic as a doorknob by its "affordances"—visual and audio clues that identify the object and suggest a manner of interaction. By designing interface elements with the affordances of everyday things, you make it easier for users to infer how they might interact with them in a multimedia context. For example, two of the most common affordances given to images to make them look "clickable" is the beveled 3-D look and the ubiquitous drop shadow.

Every destination features four postcards. Your task is to drive from city to city and find the postcards outlined in your assigned list. If you collect them all before the other players do, you win.

Once you drive to a city, the postcard-viewing interface overlays the map. Notice the thematic "dashboardlike" control panel and the straightforward way to thumb through the postcards.

MuSIC & SoUND

Music and sound can contribute immensely to interface design. Metaphors and affordances are not limited to visual clues but can also be established with sounds. Just as color and texture help us determine the physical nature of objects, the sounds associated with objects and environments help us identify them.

SOUND EFFECTS

Imagine coming across an image of a door in a multimedia title. Now imagine that when the cursor rolled over the door, a squeak sounded. What if a monster roared instead? Or, imagine hearing the faint whispers of a conversation. With these three sound effects, the same image of a door can take on three different tones: one that simply implied the door is openable, one that seemed rather threatening to click, and one that raised your curiosity and encouraged you to click it.

BACKGROUND SCORE

Most movies have elaborate musical scores that run the length of the film. Though you may not focus on it, music is always playing—even during conversation. The background score helps establish the pace of the action, sets the mood, and can even build anticipation and suspense. Multimedia designers can use music and sound effects not only to help clarify an interface, but also to add depth to a user's experience.

AGeNTS, GuIDES, & CHARaCTERS

It may seem that discussing the difference between agents, guides, and characters is like splitting hairs, but there are some important differences in how a user interacts with each and in the kind of experiences each provides. The use of "personalities" in multimedia provides a very different "feel" to the experience. Personalities can make a title seem more personalized or service-oriented, or they can add an element of humor or cynicism.

Agents Sergei and Pier Paolo of the *I/O 360 Interactive Agent* prototype provoke the user to "touch" them. They have the ability to cajole, scream, and implore the user for action. By the same token, they can be emotionally moved or hurt by the user's attention or lack thereof.

AGENTS

An agent is a character or object that carries out interactions for the user—much like a personal attendant. When a set of complex interactions is needed to accomplish something in a title, it is helpful to simply ask an agent to take care of it. This is akin to clicking on a button that automates a process, but an agent adds a friendlier tone to the experience—a sense of companionship. Also, an agent may interject personality and even learn from you, whereas a button is purely functional. I/O 360 Design has developed the I/O 360 *Interactive Agent*, a front-end user interface that employs an agent to point to a variety of interactive demos of their work. (A front-end interface is a main menu that takes you to a variety of places.)

button :

GUIDES

A guide is a simplified version of an agent that offers suggestions or help during an interaction. Help may be triggered directly by the user, or the guide may make assumptions about the user's needs and speak up on its own. While this could be a comforting feature for new users, a guide may become annoying—like a backseat driver—after a user has become familiar with the title. Therefore, providing a way to turn off the guides is often helpful to users. Apple's *Guides* 3.0 uses characters from the story to guide users through the experience. By selecting different characters, users are able to access diverse points of view on the same subject.

CHARACTERS

Characters are personalities that live within a title. On the surface, agents and guides are characters, but their expanded capabilities bring them beyond a character's role. Characters are part of the content of a title. Sometimes they

Competing for the user's attention, agents Sergei and Pier Paolo dance against a minimalist backdrop.

respond to the user's interaction (in the same way they respond to other elements and characters in the title), but mostly, they are just part of the show.

Interface functions may or may not be housed within characters. The characters of Living Books, for example, are not an integral part of the interface; they are only part of the story. Simon, the host of *The Tortoise and the Hare*, offers guidance as the host and narrator, but the user does not initiate any functions by directly interacting with him. *Wacky Jacks*, on the other hand, has users directly prompting the characters as a means of interaction.

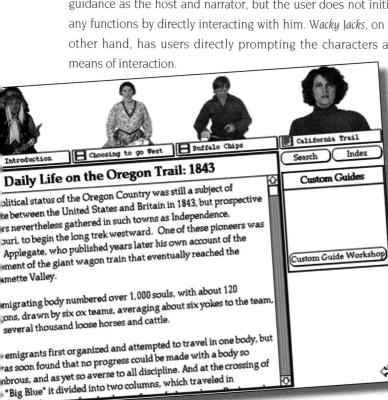

Guides 3.0, a research prototype developed at the Apple Advanced Technology Group by Abbe Don, Tim Oren, and Brenda Laurel, features American history as seen from the perspective of three guides: a Native American, a settler woman, and a frontiersman.

Ameritech has developed a prototype for interactive television that features the use of agents. Each agent represents a category of television, such as "Westerns" or "Sports." Users select an agent who then guides them through the available programming for that category.

Fish (Layer 0, RGB, 1:1)

138K/229K

Food & Wine

RECIPES   ENTREES

GOLD & SILVER

CHAPTER 5

GRAPHIC PRODUCTION
TIPS & STRATEGIES

Now that we have discussed the multimedia production process, structures, authoring tools, and user interface design, it's time to roll up our sleeves and start making multimedia. This chapter takes the theories and ideas presented so far and shows you how to actually create graphics for multimedia and online applications. It also provides methods to help you think strategically when designing multimedia.

The bridge between an inspired design and efficient production is a well-crafted and thoroughly tested prototype.

—Amy Pertschuck, C-Wave

TOOLS OF THE TRADE

Over the years a few software products have become the standard "tools of the trade" for creating multimedia imagery. Of the six software packages discussed below, three of them make up the cornerstone of multimedia graphic production: Photoshop, Illustrator, and DeBabelizer.

ADOBE PHOTOSHOP

Photoshop is the single most powerful software workhorse for creating the imagery found in most multimedia and online applications today. The depth of this program is beyond compare. Although beginners can jump in and be fairly productive, it takes months, if not years, to uncover all of Photoshop's secrets, and by then, the next version is released. Photoshop's depth can be attributed to the level of control it gives you over every aspect of an image.

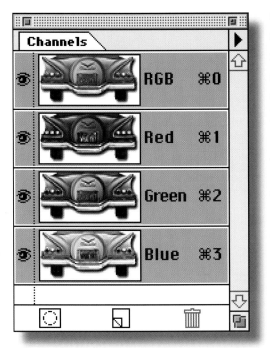

The Photoshop Channels window allows access to not only the image's color composite, but also the red, green, and blue plates that comprise the image.

In addition to allowing you to edit and manipulate an image, Photoshop allows you to access and edit all three RGB plates (see pages 96–97) that together make up an image. Photoshop compounds this control by allowing you to create layers of separate graphics—each of which has its own RGB color plate breakdown.

PHOTOSHOP'S ALPHA CHANNELS

Most of the time when editing an image, you do not want to apply changes to the entire image at once. Therefore, you need a way of isolating certain areas of an image. Photoshop provides many ways to create temporary stencils, or "friskets," in order to section off parts of an image for editing purposes. Frequently, however, these stencils take a lot of time to create; also, they are often worth saving for future uses.

For these reasons, Photoshop allows you to save grayscale representations of your stencils; they are called alpha channels.

PHOTOSHOP'S FEATURES

Photoshop's editing features include basic painting and retouching, extensive color correction, and access to a multitude of filters that do everything from image distortion to texture generation. Most importantly, these editing capabilities can be applied to isolated parts of an image (by using the stencils as described above). Lastly, Photoshop can be used to process bitmapped images into the correct dimensions and resolution, to convert vector-based images to bitmapped images, to create custom palettes, and to save images in a variety of multimedia file formats, including PICT, GIF, and BMP.

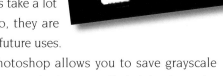

The image on the left is vector-based while the image on the right is a bitmap.

◀

By using various selection tools and techniques in Photoshop you can create temporary stencils. To keep stencils for future use, you can save them as grayscale alpha channels.

ADOBE ILLUSTRATOR

Photoshop is a bitmap-based program, meaning that you are working with images that are made up of a collection of colored pixels in a fixed resolution defined by dots per linear inch. Illustrator, on the other hand, operates in an entirely different way. Illustrator is vector-based, meaning that images are defined by points connected by lines and curves that create a mathematical outline. The advantage to this method of generating images is that you can create graphics that are resolution-independent. Because they are mathematical, vector-based images can be scaled up or down without loss of integrity—much as a square is still a square whether it is 3 x 3 millimeters or 3 x 3 miles in dimension.

The problem, however, is that multimedia does not accept vector-based graphics; they must be converted to bitmaps. Fortunately, Adobe has integrated its two products so that you can create complex, vector-based illustrations in Illustrator and then convert them to bitmaps in Photoshop (see Exercise 3, pages 84–85).

EQUILIBRIUM DEBABELIZER

As its name implies, DeBabelizer can make sense out of all kinds of image file formats, allowing you to open them up and apply conversions to them, from palette changes to file format changes. Best of all, DeBabelizer will automate these tasks. For example, you can set aside a folder of 200 images that each need to be reduced into an 8-bit palette and saved as a PICT file in another folder (see Exercise 6, pages 110–111). You can set up such a routine in DeBabelizer, click DO IT, and go to lunch!

▶

DeBabelizer's batch-processing features allow you to set up conversion routines for hundreds of images.

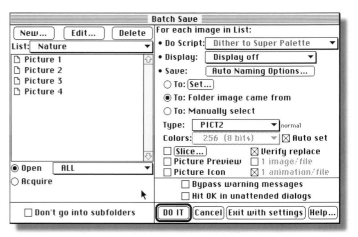

MACROMEDIA FREEHAND

FreeHand, like Illustrator, is vector-based. While many artists go back and forth comparing the capabilities of FreeHand and Illustrator, the reason that Illustrator is preferred by multimedia artists is because of its ability to integrate with Photoshop. Complex FreeHand files, when opened in Photoshop, do not always convert to bitmaps ("rasterize") with predictable results.

FRACTAL DESIGN PAINTER

Painter is a bitmap-based program like Photoshop that specializes in emulating traditional fine art media such as charcoal and oils. Because of such specialization, Painter is generally used only when fine art effects are required.

MACROMEDIA DIRECTOR

Of the tools listed so far, Director is the only one that is not used for generating and processing images into multimedia-ready graphics. As discussed in Chapter 3, Director is an authoring tool that "glues" final graphics, sound, video, and animation together to create a multimedia title. The reason I include it within this group is for its excellent prototyping abilities. Visual designers can use Director to quickly sketch their ideas in order to get a better sense of how everything comes together onscreen. These mock-ups can then be used to communicate design directions and user interface ideas to the rest of the multimedia production team.

I created this apple in Painter using the "van Gogh" brush style. I then applied a lighting effect on a paper-textured background to achieve a realistic look.

▼

HARDWƏRE

Now that we have discussed the software tools of the trade, it's time to look at my recommendations for a basic hardware configuration for multimedia designers.

COMPUTERS

For multimedia graphic production, I recommend a computer that has a relatively fast processing speed, at least 240 megabytes of hard drive space, and at least 24 megabytes of RAM (random access memory). Because multimedia graphics files are not huge in terms of dimensions and resolution, they do not take up a lot of disk space. Therefore, you can get away with the above configuration, but more RAM and more hard drive space are always useful. Most graphic designers use Macintosh computers; however, both Photoshop and Illustrator, two of the key tools of the trade, have Windows versions.

MONITORS

When shopping for a monitor, multimedia designers need to keep two things in mind. First is the size of the monitor. I recommend a monitor that's at least 17". When working on images in Photoshop, the interface windows alone take up a lot of screen space. There is nothing worse than trying to work on an image when all the interface functions are crowding the work space. Second, be sure that your monitor is capable of displaying thousands, if not millions, of colors at a time. This is related to the amount of VRAM (video random access memory) that comes standard on a computer. Often, stock computers will be able to support millions of colors on smaller monitors but not on larger 17" ones. In this case, you need to have extra VRAM installed.

REMOVABLE STORAGE

Individually, multimedia graphics files typically do not take up much disk space, but hundreds of little files together can start to take up a lot of room. Also, multimedia files are generally too large to fit on floppy disks. Because of these factors, you need some way of conveniently storing and transporting your images.

Two companies that have set the standard for removable storage are Iomega and Syquest. Iomega has offered the most cost-effective system (per megabyte of storage) to date, with both its Zip and Jazz drives. The Zip drive is a small, lightweight, portable drive that reads 100-megabyte cartridges that are the size of a floppy. The Jazz drive is also small, lightweight, and portable, but its floppy-size cartridges each hold 1 gigabyte of media.

Syquest makes a few different drives: two larger drives that support 44-megabyte and 88-megabyte cartridges, and a smaller, more portable, drive that reads 270-megabyte floppy-size cartridges. Syquest's 88-megabyte drive will read both the 88-megabyte and the 44-megabyte cartridges. Most companies and service bureaus have both Iomega and Syquest drives, so transporting your files from place to place is easy—just bring the cartridge.

TABLETS

For most people, using a mouse to maneuver around a computer system is fairly easy. When it comes to drawing, however, many artists have a difficult time using a mouse—it's like drawing with a bar of soap. Artists are often more comfortable drawing with a penlike object. Fortunately, a few companies have developed drawing tablets, which are pen-based input devices you can use instead of a mouse.

Tablets come in a variety of sizes, from 12" x 12" to 6" x 4". But, since the dimensions of the tablet map to the computer screen's dimensions, larger tablets require bigger arm movements to go from one side of the screen to the other. Larger tablets are useful, however, for tracing images. Many animators draw their images on paper, place them on the tablet, and then trace them as a way of "digitizing" them. Unless you will be doing a lot of tracing, I suggest a 9" x 6" tablet; to me, it has the best "feel."

SCANNERS

There are a variety of scanners available. Flatbed scanners are used for scanning flat images only, and slide scanners are used for scanning slides. Because multimedia does not require the use of high-resolution images, you do not need to buy a high-end scanner (such as those suitable for producing print-worthy images).

THE MuLTIMEDIA CaNVAS

Just as the constraints of technology, surfaces, and media used in traditional offset printing influence artistic decisions and require designers to deal with such issues as trapping and process color, multimedia presents its own set of constraints and issues.

ONSCREEN RESOLUTION

Regardless of an image's resolution, the computer screen has a fixed number of "slots" in which to display pixels—generally 72 slots per linear inch (referred to as "72 dpi," dots per inch). Images with a higher resolution than 72 dpi have more "dots" per inch than there are "slots" per inch in the monitor. Therefore, in order to physically display all the pixel information of a high-resolution image, the computer must "enlarge" it. This is why high-resolution images, when viewed on a computer screen, appear to be larger than they actually are. On the other hand, 72-dpi images will be displayed at their actual size because there is a one-to-one mapping of image pixels per inch to monitor slots per inch.

IMAGE SIZE VERSUS RESOLUTION

Because images that are not 72 dpi are displayed according to their resolution rather than their actual size, a quick way in Photoshop to get a sense of an image's true size is to click and hold in the lower left corner of the document's window. A pop-up thumbnail shows you how your image (represented as a picture box) relates to a standard 8.5" x 11" page.

MATCHING IMAGE AND MONITOR RESOLUTION

When designing onscreen graphics, it almost goes without saying that the resolution of your images should match the resolution of the display monitor. High-resolution images are useless in a multimedia context because, as described above, the computer monitor cannot physically display them.

SCREEN DIMENSIONS

Another factor to keep in mind is screen dimensions. For purely market reasons, most multimedia and online applications today are designed for the ubiquitous 13" color monitor. Consumers do not usually buy the larger 17" and 21" monitors, so in order to reach the largest audience, you need to design multimedia products that fit within the confines of the smaller monitors. There is nothing to prevent you, however, from designing multimedia for a larger monitor—it depends on your audience. Whichever monitor size you choose to design for, be sure to make your graphics and backgrounds match its dimensions.

The above grid illustrates how a computer monitor works. A fixed-size grid houses the colored pixels that make up an image onscreen. The above image has a dot size that matches the grid's square size. Therefore, for every pixel of color, there is a corresponding slot on the grid and the image is displayed at its actual size.

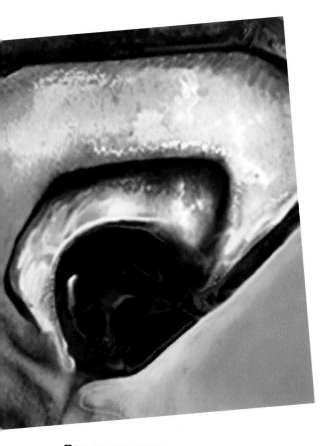

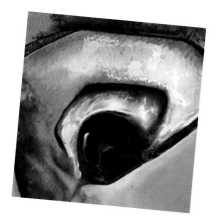

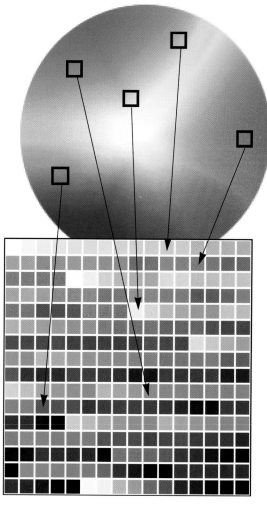

COLOR PALETTE

The color spectrum of the RGB computer screen encompasses millions of color possibilities (see pages 96–97). Unfortunately, however, it takes processing power to display all the millions of colors at once. Most consumer monitors do not come equipped with the extra VRAM (video random access memory) it takes to show more than 256 colors on the screen at one time. Therefore, in order to reach the largest audience, multimedia titles need to be designed with a color palette limited to 256 colors. As ugly as that sounds, there are ways to use color palettes to get the best-looking results (see Chapter 6, "Understanding Color and Palettes").

Two images of the same dimension will appear at different sizes onscreen in Photoshop if their resolution is different. The image on the left is 150 dpi, and the image on the right is 72 dpi. The size difference is due to the fixed pixel size of a monitor's display. Since high-resolution images pack more dots into the same space, Photoshop must enlarge the images to show you all their pixels.

Out of a pool of 16 million colors, 8-bit monitors can display a palette of only 256 colors at a time.

IMaGE CaPTURE

Unless you are going to create graphics from scratch on the computer, you need to be familiar with the various ways to capture images into the computer.

SCANNING

The most common way to digitize images, of course, is through the use of a scanner. There are two types of scanners: flatbed scanners that scan flat imagery as well as 3-D objects, such as pencils, placed on the scanning bed (although results for 3-D objects are less predictable), and slide scanners that specialize in digitizing transparencies.

SCANNING TIPS

When scanning color images on a flatbed scanner, it is best to scan in 24-bit color (see pages 98–99) and at 150 dpi. A good rule of thumb is to scan at twice the resolution of your target. In multimedia, your target resolution is usually 72 dpi, so scanning at 150 dpi is about right. One word of caution, however: This rule applies only when the size of the image you are scanning is the correct size or larger. If you need to enlarge the image, then you should scan at a higher resolution. For instance, if you are scanning a small photograph and need it to be twice as large, then double the scanning rule, too: 2 x 150 dpi = 300 dpi. If the image needs to be three times as large, scan at 450 dpi, and so on (be aware, however, that scanning such small originals will affect quality).

REDUCING IMAGE RESOLUTION

It is always best to capture as large an image as possible in the scanning process and then reduce the resolution with a tool like Photoshop. The process of reducing resolution usually gets rid of unwanted moiré patterns and dust, and also tends to sharpen up the edges and meld colors together. A large original scan gives you more options when it comes to downsizing your image.

AVOIDING INTERPOLATION

What you want to avoid at all costs is bumping images up to a higher resolution (enlarging images). The degeneration is considerable because the process of enlarging an image's dimensions or resolution arbitrarily inserts pixels where there were none before. This process, called interpolation, essentially guesses what the color of the new pixels should be by averaging the value of neighboring pixels. Such averaging of color values causes an image to appear blurred.

VIDEO CAPTURE

Because video cameras are designed to capture moving images, it is difficult to get sharp still images from a video capture. Also keep in mind that video resolution is not as good as the computer screen's, and video color is less saturated.

With that said, video capture can be very useful for creating animation. For instance, Kaleida's *Monterey Canyon* features a

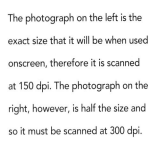

The photograph on the left is the exact size that it will be when used onscreen, therefore it is scanned at 150 dpi. The photograph on the right, however, is half the size and so it must be scanned at 300 dpi.

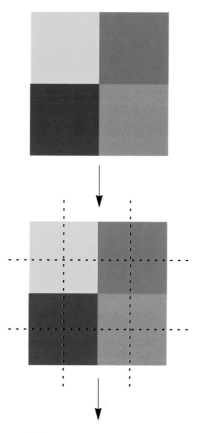

seagull guide that takes you from place to place. To create the animation, I videotaped seagulls flying around, digitized the video, then pieced together the flight of various birds into one realistic sequence. Using Photoshop, I stripped out the backgrounds and fixed up each frame, adjusting the color and painting in the details. The result was a realistic controlled animation of a seagull.

Tools like Adobe Premiere are excellent for capturing and editing video to create both animations, like the above seagull, and onscreen movies.

The interpolation process of enlarging an image by a factor of two works by "drawing and quartering" each pixel. Four new pixels are created from one by slightly blending its quadrants with neighboring quadrants. The result, as shown below, is a slightly blurred version of the original.

Kaleida's *Monterey Canyon* seagull animation is a collection of sequences that are strung together in ScriptX. All frames were hand-selected from hundreds of video frames to piece together a controlled animation.

GRAPHIC LAYeRS

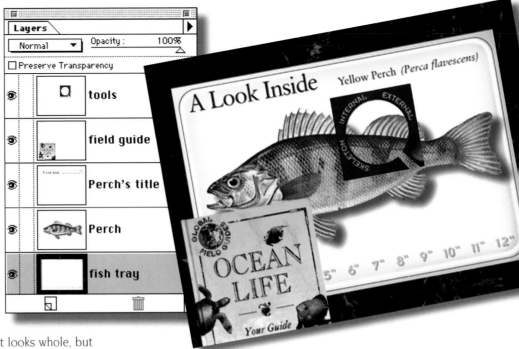

Multimedia is a dynamic, ever-changing environment. In order to achieve maximum flexibility and dynamic control, it's best to keep the graphic elements comprising a multimedia title as separate files. Authoring tools create a composite effect by layering the various graphic elements on top of each other. The net result is an image that looks whole, but in reality is made up of multiple graphic images. By layering, you can make individual images move around, animate when the cursor rolls over them, or disappear altogether.

For instance, imagine creating a self-promotional multimedia presentation. If you want your name and logo to fade up from an image of your work, you need to keep your name and logo as a separate file from your portfolio image. If you wanted to fade up just your logo, and then your name, you would have to separate the logo and name into two files. The more you keep graphic elements separate from one another, the more theatrical control you can have.

TWO TYPES OF LAYERS

You can create two kinds of graphic layers for multimedia: layers that use the "blue screen" effect to achieve a transparent background and layers of images that have been rendered to the background and then cut out.

Transparent layers are created by selecting one solid color and designating it as the transparent color. This type of layer is used for images that will move around onscreen (see pages 72–73).

Cutout layers are created by combining an image with the background and then cutting it out and saving it as a separate file. This way it matches the background perfectly when overlaid, and the image can be anti-aliased to that portion of the background (see pages 74–75).

FEEDBACK

Layers are often used to give feedback. When a user rolls over a hot spot, the graphic can "highlight" by temporarily overlaying an altered version of itself. Then when the user clicks, a third version of the graphic can briefly appear. This multiple-state graphic, made up of a set of layers, is a common convention used in multimedia (see pages 78–79).

Kaleida's *Monterey Canyon* lab section consists of a few different layers: a lab tray, a fish, the fish's title, the field guide, and various examination tools.

The Photoshop Layers window (shown at far left) indicates how the lab section's component graphics are stacked on top of each other.

BACKGROUND GRAPHIC

When designing a multimedia screen, the first element to consider is the backdrop. Throughout the various places of a multimedia title, there is generally a background that does not change. You need to determine what belongs on the backdrop and what should be kept as a separate file, or layer.

To do this, figure out which graphic elements are going to be temporal (sometimes there, sometimes not), animated (including buttons with highlight states), or mobile (moving around onscreen). With a few exceptions, these elements should not be a part of your background, but should be saved as separate files.

PHOTOSHOP LAYERS

Photoshop gives you the ability to simulate the graphic layering that will occur in authoring tools. This is a useful feature for multimedia artists because you can see the interrelationships among individual graphics as you are working on them. But Photoshop layers are only useful while

you are working. Once you have finished creating the images and are ready to integrate them into an authoring tool, you need to copy each layer into its own separate file, since authoring tools do not read layered Photoshop documents.

Also keep in mind that Photoshop supports true transparent layers whereas authoring tools do not. In order to achieve transparency in an authoring tool, you need to assign one color as the "transparent" color (see pages 72–73).

The character sitting in the chair of KidSoft's Clubroom has been combined with a piece of the background, then cut out and used as an overlay.

The fish of Kaleida's *Monterey Canyon* had a transparent key color as their background so that they could swim around, layered on top of an animated undersea environment.

Key Color Transparency

Unlike Photoshop, authoring tools do not support true transparency, but rely instead on the "blue screen" technique. This technique designates one solid color as the key color, or transparent color (also called the "chroma key").

There are two situations that require the use of key color transparency: when images are moving around against a nonuniform background or when a background is changing behind an image. For instance, if an object is moving across a solid white background, there is no need to use a key color—simply fill the image's surrounding area with solid white so that it will match.

Video tools like Adobe Premiere not only support key color transparency, but also alpha channel transparency (see illustration on page 99).

RULES
When using key color transparency in graphic overlays, there are a few rules to keep in mind.

1) The background surrounding your image must be a single solid color. Any background pixels of a varying color will not become transparent and will remain onscreen along with the image.

2) The key color must be selected from within the color palette you are using for the image. You cannot arbitrarily choose a color from the entire range of possible colors. But be aware that you must choose a color from the palette that the image is not using. For example, when creating a palette, include one color that will be used only as a key color. This is why artists often use "video blue" as a key color—it's not a color commonly found within images.

3) Lastly, make sure that your image's outer edge is aliased! If your image is anti-aliased to the key color, you will see a rim around your image (I call it "cheese," but it's generally referred to as "artifacts"; see pages 74–75). Since only one color can be transparent, the anti-aliased in-between colors are left opaque. There is one exception to this rule. You can anti-alias an image to a key color that closely matches the overall color and tone of the background. Therefore, the artifacts will not be as noticeable. I only recommend this, however, for short, controlled segments.

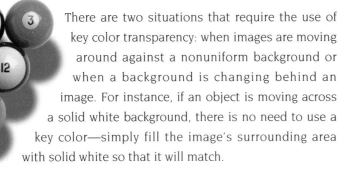

The white surrounding the 8 ball will be included when the image is overlaid. The computer has no way of knowing that the white is nonessential. In order for the white to become transparent, you need to designate it as the key color, or use the matte ink effect.

Matte ink effect

Most authoring tools allow you to use the default white background, surrounding an image, as a transparent matte. Unlike using a key color, the "matte ink effect," as it is called, does not affect white pixels in the interior of an image. Therefore, the white background area will become transparent, while any white pixels inside the image will remain white. For instance, the 8 ball at far left could use the white matte ink effect to key out its white surrounding area without affecting the interior white colors.

A key color must be chosen from one of the colors in your palette (shown at far left). A key color must be a single flat color. If there are even slight variations in color, those variant pixels will not become transparent.

2Market, a CD-ROM shopping catalog, uses a QuickTime video of a woman, shot against a blue screen, to achieve the effect of the woman walking around in the interface.

ANTI-ALIASED & ALIASED GRAPHICS

Since an image is made up of pixels and pixels are square, the edges of computer images look jagged. Such a jagged appearance is most noticeable on the curves of images—they look like stairsteps. That type of rough, jagged edge is referred to as an "aliased" edge.

To avoid the stairstepping and soften an image's appearance, you can use a technique known as "anti-aliasing." Anti-aliasing slightly blends the edges of an image into its surroundings so that your eye perceives smoother, more natural edges.

PROBLEMS WITH ANTI-ALIASED OVERLAYS

Since anti-aliasing blends two colored edges together, the result is a series of in-between colors that create a smooth transition from one color to the other. If the image is then moved on top of a different color—especially one that is lighter or darker—the previous anti-aliasing will not match. The in-between colors around the rim of the image (called "artifacts") will stand out dramatically.

For example, if an image is anti-aliased to a white background, the rim of the image becomes a pastel in-between color combining the color of the image and the white background. While the image looks good overlaid on a white background and even on other light-colored backgrounds, it will not look good overlaid on a dark background.

BEST USES FOR ANTI-ALIASED GRAPHICS

Anti-aliased graphics are safe to use when you know that the background behind an image will remain constant or that the image will not be moving around onscreen. For instance, if a layer of text fades in onscreen against a certain background and does not move, it is safe to anti-alias the text to that background. But if the background will change underneath the text layer, you need to create a new text layer to match—anti-aliased to the new background.

To create an anti-aliased layer for a multimedia project, simply combine the image with the background where it will appear and cut it out. Since the cutout matches the background perfectly, all the eye sees when it is overlaid is the image within, nicely anti-aliased.

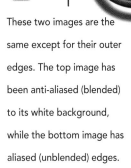

These two images are the same except for their outer edges. The top image has been anti-aliased (blended) to its white background, while the bottom image has aliased (unblended) edges.

On the other hand, the aliased image looks fine against both light-colored and dark-colored backgrounds. This is why it is important to use aliased edges when an image will be moving across a variety of backgrounds.

The image that has been anti-aliased to white looks fine against a white background (left side). When placed against a dark-colored background, however, the image dramatically reveals the pastel-colored artifacts created by blending the image to white (right side).

If the seagull of Kaleida's *Monterey Canyon* had been anti-aliased to the blue key color, just imagine the blue rim of artifacts it would have as it flew through the various scenes.

Photoshop anti-aliased layers

When you use Photoshop's layering feature, often you'll choose anti-aliased edges for your images. But because the images are anti-aliased to true transparency, the edges are not blended to any one color, but merely fade out. Therefore, graphic layers in Photoshop, though anti-aliased, look good over all types of colored backgrounds. Authoring tools, however, must use a key color to achieve transparency. Therefore, you need to get rid of the anti-aliased edges and fill the transparency with a solid key color. A quick way to do this is detailed in Exercise 1 on pages 76–77.

Use aliased graphics for key color overlays

As unattractive as aliased graphics are, they come in handy when creating layers that use key color transparency. Since only one color can be transparent, the key color should be nestled up directly against the edge of an image. If an image has been anti-aliased to the key color, the in-between colors will not become transparent but will remain as a rim of artifacts. Imagine if the seagull on pages 68–69 were anti-aliased to the blue key color. When the blue is keyed out, the semi-blue blended edges would remain along with the bird.

EXERCISE 1
CONVERTING ANTI-ALIASED to ALIASED

In order to use key color transparency properly, images must have aliased edges. However, the process of converting anti-aliased images into aliased images can be a daunting task. Just imagine zooming into the edges of an image and manually painting out the anti-aliasing! Fortunately, there are a few tricks you can do in Photoshop to quickly convert anti-aliased images into aliased images.

NOTE:

This exercise assumes that the image to be processed is an anti-aliased image on a transparent layer. If your image is anti-aliased to a color, then select it with the selection tools, copy it before you start this exercise, and skip to Step 2.

A close-up reveals the anti-aliased edges of the fish on a transparent background.

STEP 1

Make sure that the layer in Photoshop that contains your image is active. Choose Select All from the Select menu, and copy the contents. Because the image is on a transparent layer, only the image will be copied.

STEP 2

Set up a new file (set the background contents to white) and paste the image into it—notice how the selection has shrunk to fit your image automatically. Do not let go of the selection once the image is pasted. While the selection is still active, choose Save Selection from the Select menu. This will turn the selection into a grayscale "alpha channel," or stencil. Now that the selection is saved, choose None from the Select menu to deselect the image (very important).

STEP 3

Go to the new alpha channel you have just created. Notice the gray pixels between the black and the white ones. These gray pixels represent the anti-aliased edges of your image. To get rid of all gray pixels in the channel, choose Map: Threshold from the Image menu. The default setting that appears is fine; click OK.

Turn channels into active selections again by dragging their icon down to the lower left icon. To duplicate a channel, drag it to the lower middle icon.

You now have an aliased channel that is the shape of your image. Before you continue, duplicate this channel (#4) by clicking on its title and dragging down to the middle icon at the bottom of the Channels window. (We will save this original (#4) for later to demonstrate another way to get rid of anti-aliasing.)

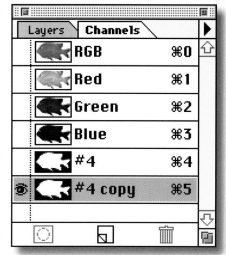

Layers	Channels	▶
🐟 RGB	⌘0
🐟 Red	⌘1
🐟 Green	⌘2
🐟 Blue	⌘3
🐟 #4	⌘4
🐟 #4 copy	⌘5

STEP 4

Turn the copied alpha channel (#4 copy) into a selection (as shown above) and then go back to the color image. You will notice that the selection passes through the middle of the image's anti-aliasing. Therefore, not only do you need to fill the outside of the selection with a solid key color, you also need to fix up the image on the inside of the selection.

STEP 5

From the Select menu, choose Select Inverse to select the background area. Fill the background with a key color (remember to choose a key color from the 256-color palette you will be using, and be sure that the color is not used inside the image). Choose Select Inverse again so that your image is selected.

The active selection runs down the center of the anti-aliasing so that even if you correct the outer pastel rim, you will still need to correct the inside almost-orange pixels.

STEP 6

Choose Float from the Select menu. This lifts your image off the page, giving you access to the Matting commands found in the Select menu. Choose Matting: Defringe…, enter a width of 1 pixel, and click OK. That's it, you now have an aliased image on a solid key-colored background.

ALTERNATE METHOD

Another way to get rid of the anti-aliased edges is to contract the size of either the alpha channel or the selection by 1 pixel. This selects the image on the inside of its anti-aliasing. By choosing Inverse from the Select menu and filling with a key color, all anti-aliasing is removed.

CONTRACTING A CHANNEL

Go to the original alpha channel, and under the Filter menu, choose Other: Minimum. Enter in a radius of 1 pixel and click OK. Turn this channel into a selection and repeat Step 5.

CONTRACTING A SELECTION

Turn the original alpha channel into a selection. Under the Select menu, choose Modify: Contract… and enter a value of 1 pixel. Now repeat Step 5.

Contracting the selection by one pixel all around clips the image to the inside of the anti-aliasing.

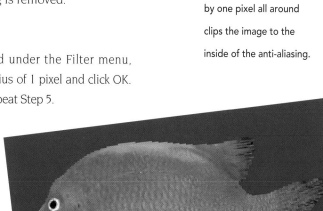

The final aliased-edge fish set on a solid key color background looks like this.

FL₆I̧P B₆₆KS

All frames of the alarm clock flip book are registered because they share the same dimension, but notice all the wasted space in the upper right portion.

A flip book is a series of graphic layers that together comprise an animation. Often, multimedia titles will use flip books, instead of movies, to create animations. Not only are flip books easier to create and process than movies, but they also take up less disk space. Another factor to consider is that computers cannot support fast frame rates for movies—certainly not 30 frames per second, as is the standard for broadcast video—so flip books provide a good alternative. You can create a flip book that loops around only 3 frames, or you can create one that quickly flips through 20 frames.

TWO TYPES OF FLIP BOOKS

Since a flip book is a collection of layers, authoring tools treat flip books the same way they treat layers. Therefore, just as there are two types of graphic layers, there are also two kinds of flip books—ones that use key color transparency and ones that are cutouts.

SAME DIMENSIONS

Ideally, a flip book should be composed of a series of images that are exactly the same dimensions. This makes registration easier in an authoring tool and gives you the

option of making the series into a movie if you ever need to. The way to make the series of images all the same size is to identify the minimum amount of space needed by the sequence and crop each image in the series accordingly (see example above). Any extraneous space you can crop out reduces the flip book's file size and increases the speed of the animation.

One drawback, however, to having all images in a series be the same dimensions is that you often end up with wasted space on a lot of the frames. For instance, if you were to animate a logo so that it revolves in a circular motion, each frame would position the logo near one of the edges, leaving the surrounding area as wasted, but necessary, space so that the frames would be registered to each other (see Exercise 2, pages 80–81). There is a way to avoid such wasted space, and it has to do with the way graphic layers and flip books are positioned onscreen by an authoring tool (see below).

X, Y LOCATION

Authoring tools position overlays onscreen by using an X and Y axis coordinate system. A 13″ monitor has a screen dimension of 640 pixels along the X axis (width) and 480 pixels along the Y axis

Using selected frames from Eadweard Muybridge's photographs as a guide, I created a nine-frame flip book that loops to create a cantering horse.

(height). Unlike a traditional X and Y grid, however, a computer counts from 0,0 starting in the upper left corner of the screen.

Images are placed onscreen according to where their upper left corner is located on the X and Y grid; this is referred to as an image's "X, Y location." Therefore, the important registration point of a flip book series is the upper left corner. Rather than keeping a series the same dimensions, and in order to save disk space, extraneous space on the bottom right corner of images can be cropped out. Be aware, however, that while cropping the series may save disk space, the lack of uniform size among the images may make registration difficult in some authoring tools. For instance, Director has layering features that work well for a series of images that are all the same dimension.

MOBILE FLIP BOOKS
Once a flip book is created from a series of images registered to each other (either by maintaining the same upper left corner or by maintaining the same dimensions), it does not have to be placed onscreen at one static X, Y location. It can become a

mobile unit, moving around the screen while flipping through its frames. The seagull animation (shown on pages 68–69), for instance, is a flip book that "flies" around the screen.

MULTIPLE-STATE GRAPHICS
The various frames of a flip book can give users feedback in a multimedia title. For example, the first state, or resting state, would be frame one. When the user rolled over the area, frame two would appear as a highlight, and when the user clicked, frame three would appear as another altered graphic.

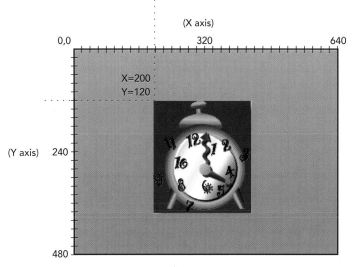

(X axis)

0,0   320   640

X=200
Y=120

(Y axis)   240

480

Rather than keeping the images of a flip book the same dimension, you can crop out their lower right corners up to the image. This way you save file space while preserving the upper left registration corner.

Images are positioned onscreen by the X and Y coordinates of their upper left corner. Though this image is using a key color, the color still counts as size information and therefore affects the X, Y location.

EXERCISE 2
CReATING FLiP BooKS

An easy way to create a flip book is to use the Photoshop layering feature. By using each layer to store a different frame of animation, you can quickly see how all the frames interrelate. Also, because you can create all the frames together in one document, registration is easy. In this exercise, you will create a simple five-frame animation of an object revolving in a circular pattern.

STEP 1

Find a small image, about 100 x 100 pixels, and open it in Photoshop. Make sure that the image is on a transparent background. Enlarge the canvas size (located under the Image menu) so that the image has room to animate in a circular pattern.

STEP 2

Duplicate the layer four times (shown at left) and rename the duplicates "Layer 1," "Layer 2," etc.

STEP 3

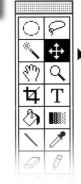

Using the Move tool, click on each layer individually and reposition each of the images so that in sequence they move around in a circle.

STEP 4

If you do not use the entire canvas size and you have unused space surrounding your animation, crop the file to the smallest area possible (shown above). This minimizes the amount of disk space that your animation requires.

STEP 5

Now that you have a series of five layers, positioned to create a circular animation and cropped to occupy the smallest space, you now need to copy each layer and save it as its own file. (Authoring tools will not read a layered Photoshop document.) Copying a transparent layer, however, copies only the image and crops out the transparent background. But since the transparent background is holding the image in place relative to the other images, you need to replace the transparency with a solid color or background before you copy the layers.

To do this, create a new layer by clicking on the lower left icon in the Layers window. Either fill the new layer with a solid color (that you could use as a key color) or with a portion of the background graphic.

By clicking on the layer's title and dragging it to the lower left icon, you create a duplicate of the layer. By clicking solely on the lower left icon, you create a new, blank layer. To rename a layer, double click on its title.

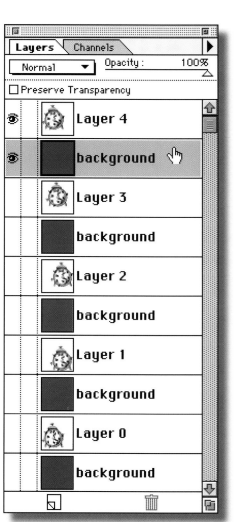

The arrow icon on the upper right of the Layers window has a pull-down menu that contains the Merge Layers function. Before merging, choose the layers you want to merge by turning on their eyeballs and by selecting one of them. Make sure the other layers' eyeballs are turned off.

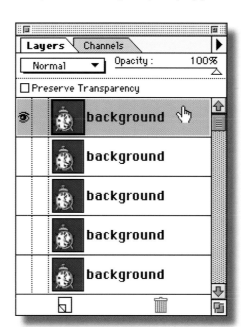

STEP 6

Duplicate the background four times so that there is one for each frame of animation (shown at left). Reposition the background layers, inserting one between each animation frame so that each has its own background.

STEP 7

Now merge each animation layer with its background layer. To do this, turn off all the eyeballs (by clicking once on them) except for the two next to the layers you want to merge. Also, make sure that one of the layers to merge is selected (in gray). Choose the Merge Layers function from the pull-down menu at the top of the Layers window. Do this for each pair of background and animation frames so that you end up with five composited animation frames.

STEP 8

Select each frame individually and copy it into its own new file. (Note: When you set up a new file, the dialog box asks you what the background "contents" should be; select White or Background Color, not Transparent.) Lastly, reduce each file's palette (see page 102), and save the files as PICT or BMP files. You now have a flip book of five frames; import the frames individually into an authoring tool, "wire" them together, and play your animation.

TYP⊙GRAPHY

A PostScript font's mathematical, vector-based outline is stored in its printer font.

As a multimedia designer, it is important to understand the way fonts work on the computer and how they are used in multimedia. Not only are there different font formats, but there are also different ways to represent type on the screen. These factors become significant when distributing multimedia and online applications. For instance, sometimes a multimedia title requires that end users have special fonts installed on their computer.

included in the screen font's collection, the font will appear as an enlarged, pixilated mess. To remedy this, you can use Adobe Type Manager (ATM), a utility application that accesses the font's outline in the printer font, to scale the onscreen type to the desired size.

TrueType is Apple's proprietary font format. The advantage to TrueType is that you only need the one file in order to use the font. Also, you do not need an application like ATM to access the font's outline when scaling the font to various sizes.

POSTSCRIPT AND TRUETYPE

There are two standard font formats available for the computer: Adobe's PostScript format and Apple's TrueType format.

There are two files you need to have on your computer in order to use PostScript fonts properly—the screen font and the printer font. You can tell them apart by their icons. The screen font, which usually has a suitcase icon, is a collection of bitmaps of the font precut to various point sizes, generally 10, 12, 14, 18, and 24 points. The printer font, which usually has the letter A on its icon, is a vector-based, mathematical outline of the font. If you set type in point sizes other than those

READING TEXT ONSCREEN

User tests have shown that, in a multimedia context, people will not read a lot of text on the screen. Scrolling fields of text set in 12-point type with tight leading (the space between lines) are almost always glossed over. While many multimedia developers insist on providing as much information as possible, most of their efforts are for naught. Like writing text for the television screen, writing for multimedia should be concise and limited. But if there is a lot of text onscreen, be sure to use ample leading. In addition, keep the length of each line under 3". The reader's eyes can get lost finding the next line if the lines are too long.

The above pagelike icons with a single "A" indicate a single PostScript or TrueType screen font. The suitcase icons work like folders and contain more than one screen font (suitcase icons are used by both PostScript and TrueType fonts). Icons with three "A"s indicate a collection of TrueType fonts.

The icons at left are PostScript printer font icons. TrueType fonts, unlike PostScript fonts, do not need two kinds of files per font in order to work properly.

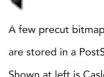

A few precut bitmaps at various point sizes are stored in a PostScript font's screen font. Shown at left is Caslon 540 Roman at 10, 16, and 18 points (enlarged to show detail).

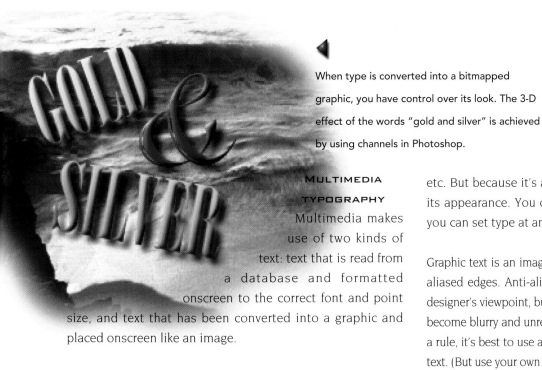

When type is converted into a bitmapped graphic, you have control over its look. The 3-D effect of the words "gold and silver" is achieved by using channels in Photoshop.

MULTIMEDIA TYPOGRAPHY

Multimedia makes use of two kinds of text: text that is read from a database and formatted onscreen to the correct font and point size, and text that has been converted into a graphic and placed onscreen like an image.

DATABASE TEXT

Multimedia titles can read text files, stored in a database, and place them into "text fields" onscreen where they are formatted, assigned a typeface, and sized. Because they are true text files, they can be edited, and their point size and leading can be changed. The problem, however, is that most multimedia authoring tools give designers poor control over text formatting. Database text is aliased and is always on a straight grid. Also, when you assign fonts to text fields, those fonts need to be available on the host computer or the text field will use a default font. Since most consumers do not have a variety of fonts, you need to include any nonstandard fonts along with the multimedia application.

GRAPHIC TEXT

Once text has been converted into a graphic, it loses its text properties; it can no longer be edited, checked for spelling,

etc. But because it's a graphic, you have greater control over its appearance. You can create curved and distorted text, or you can set type at an angle.

Graphic text is an image and so it can have either aliased or anti-aliased edges. Anti-aliased text generally looks the best from a designer's viewpoint, but thin type or type that is set too small will become blurry and unreadable when it's anti-aliased. Therefore, as a rule, it's best to use at least 12-point type in anti-aliased graphic text. (But use your own judgment, as all fonts vary.)

Anti-aliased graphic text, however, is rarely practical when extensive text is needed in a multimedia title. Unless you are willing to convert lengthy text into bitmaps, you are stuck with aliased database text.

Sumeria's *Wild Africa* uses graphic text in order to control the layout of text and images. When a title uses database text, however, text flows into a text field onscreen, which cannot be controlled as easily. When there is more database text than there is room on the screen, designers must either use a standard scrolling field or devise another user interface for browsing through text.

EXERCISE 3
INTEGRATING ILLUSTRATOR & PHOTOSHOP

The above image is the original Illustrator file that I used to create the KidSoft dungeon Clubroom. Note the "placed" Photoshop dungeon background, originally from Davidson's *Flying Colors*, that I used as a template.

Because Photoshop and Illustrator work so well together, I often create entire graphic scenes in Illustrator and then bring them into Photoshop for final processing. For instance, the KidSoft dungeon Clubroom was made by placing a Photoshop background in Illustrator and then using it as a template to create the room's furniture. Once created, the furniture was then brought into Photoshop and combined with the background template.

Though not as complex as the above example, this exercise uses the same procedure to create typographic elements that are molded to a Photoshop image.

NOTE:
This exercise assumes that you have a basic familiarity with Illustrator, especially drawing Bézier curves and creating type.

STEP 1
Find a Photoshop image with interesting contours that would be nicely augmented by a decorative text path. Open the image in Photoshop, "flatten" it by choosing Flatten Layers in the Layers window pull-down menu, and strip out all of its alpha channels. Then choose Save As… from the File menu and save the image as an EPS file. Quit Photoshop unless you have enough memory to have both Photoshop and Illustrator open at the same time.

STEP 2
Launch Illustrator. Since Illustrator is able to place EPS files from Photoshop, you can use these images as templates. Under the File menu, choose Place Art…; locate your Photoshop EPS file and click Open.

STEP 3
Lock the template in place so that you do not accidentally move it. Choose Lock from the Arrange menu.

Using either the Freehand Drawing tool or the Pen tool, create a path that follows the contour of the image. Create the path where you would like to wrap text. This path will become the baseline of the text.

You can tell if a Photoshop image is flattened by its italicized layer name (such as *Background*, shown at left). To flatten an image, click on the upper right arrow of the Layers window. In the pull-down menu that appears, choose Flatten Layers.

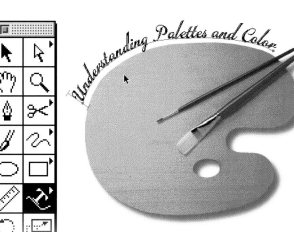

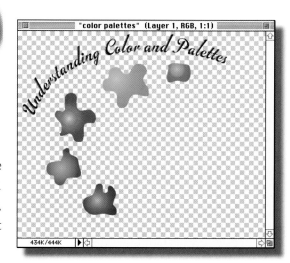

"color palettes" (Layer 1, RGB, 1:1)

Understanding Color and Palettes

434K/444K

To create a path, use either the Pen tool or the Freehand Drawing tool.

Once you have created a path, select the Text on Paths typing tool, and click on the part of the path where you would like to begin typing.

STEP 4

Now select the Text on Paths typing tool. (By clicking and holding down on the Text tool, a palette of three text tools appears; select the Text on Paths tool.) Bring the tool over to the beginning of your path and click on it. The path should disappear and a flashing cursor should appear. Type in your text.

STEP 5

Change the font and point size of the text until you have the right proportions in relation to your image.

STEP 6

If you were to save this Illustrator file and open it in Photoshop, be aware that Photoshop would only import the text portion, not the graphic EPS template. This is fine except for the fact that the text has been carefully registered to a certain area of the graphic. Since Photoshop assumes that everything else in the Illustrator file is transparent, it will only import the cropped text.

The way to preserve your registration is to create a rectangle the size of the template and use it as your cropmarks. An easy way to create a rectangle to the exact dimensions of your image is to first set your Illustrator preferences to points and pixels as the unit of measurement (under Preferences: General in the File menu). Then, using the Rectangle tool,

click once onscreen. A dialog box will ask for the dimensions. Enter in the dimensions and click OK. Position the new rectangle precisely over the template, fill it with transparency, and give it a black outline so that you can see where to position it over your image.

STEP 7

While the rectangle is still selected, turn it into cropmarks by choosing Cropmarks: Make from the Object pull-down menu.

STEP 8

Save this file as a regular Illustrator file, quit Illustrator, and open the file in Photoshop. When you do this, Photoshop will ask you how you want to rasterize the image (convert it from a vector-based graphic into a bitmap). You can choose to have the text either aliased or anti-aliased, you can specify the resolution, and you can enter in any dimensional change (since you created the file to be the correct size, don't change the dimensions).

When the image comes up, notice that Photoshop recognized the cropmarks you set in Illustrator. You now have text on a transparent layer that is sized, positioned, and molded to your original background image, ready to be combined.

By setting cropmarks in Illustrator, the text comes into Photoshop sized and positioned correctly. Simply combine it with the original palette image and add finishing touches.

FILE MANAGEMENT

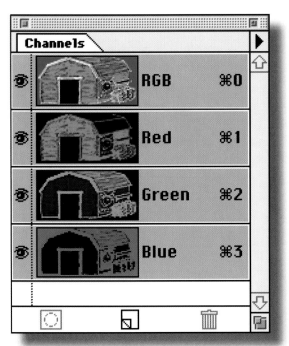

To save a Photoshop image as a PICT, BMP, GIFF, or JPEG file, it must first be flattened and have no alpha channels other than its RGB channels.

There are certain conventions for managing multimedia graphics files. Not only are there various file formats that you must use, but there are also file name and file size considerations to keep in mind.

MULTIMEDIA FILE FORMATS

Final art for multimedia needs to be saved in either the PICT file format (for Macintosh) or the BMP file format (for Windows). If you are using Photoshop to process your images, you cannot save an image as either a PICT or a BMP file if it has more than one alpha channel, or if its layers have not been "flattened." Even though the PICT file format can save one alpha channel, it's best to throw away all channels so that the image will take up less disk space. The less space an image takes up, the faster it can load onto the screen.

Always save a copy of your original 24-bit Photoshop file, with its layers and channels, as a backup source file. Then, on another copy, flatten the layers, throw away the channels, and reduce the palette. Choose Save As… from the File menu, give the file a new name, and select the PICT or BMP file format.

ONLINE FILE FORMATS

Final graphics for online applications use two different file formats, GIFF and JPEG. Both of these formats compress graphics so that they can travel faster over the Internet and download quickly on the end user's screen. The JPEG file format, however, only works for 24-bit graphics. Therefore, JPEG graphics will take up more disk space than their 8-bit counterparts. But the JPEG format allows you to have 24-bit graphics on a Web site.

The GIFF file format significantly compresses 8-bit graphics. For this reason, it is the file format most often used for online graphics. One thing to consider, however, is that the GIFF format does not compress complex photographic-like images very well. For instance, the clouds on the MCI Web site, though limited in color palette, did not compress well and so were used sparingly onscreen.

FILE NAMES

When designing a Macintosh multimedia title, your files do not need to adhere to any special naming conventions. But if you are designing a title to be cross-platform, namely to work on both Mac and Windows, then file names become an issue. Windows 3.1 requires that a file name not exceed eight characters and not contain spaces, such as "FlghtSim."

Photographic images do not compress very well when saved in the GIFF file format, which is the format most often used for online graphics.

Clubroom.dir

After the eight-character file name, you can add a period followed by a three-character "extension" that helps to identify the file. For instance, a Director movie is defined by ".dir," and a picture is defined by ".pic."

Clubroom.pic

Since using only eight characters in a name makes describing files difficult, it's a good practice for everyone to agree on a naming convention. For instance, the graphics for each section of a title might be coded by a standard first capital letter.

Because you cannot use any spaces in a Windows 3.1 file name, many people use an underscore instead.

FILE SIZE

One thing to always keep in mind when designing for multimedia is the size of your files in terms of megabytes. A full-screen 9" x 6.5" (640 pixels x 480 pixels) image is 900K in 24-bit color, 400K in 16-bit color, and 300K in 8-bit color. The time it takes to load just one of these full-screen files and then add graphic overlays, sound, and video, could be unbearable for today's audience.

BREAKING LARGE FILES INTO TILES

A trick to handling large images is to break them up into smaller tiles that can be pieced together by software. We designed the cyclorama landscape of *Playfarm* in precisely this manner. The actual landscape is a cylinder 3,600 pixels wide x 480 pixels high. An image of that size would take a lot of computing power to load intact, so we cut it up into tiles only 120 pixels wide. This way, only the tiles currently in view need to be loaded into memory. Tiles just offscreen are preloaded to make panning quick and easy.

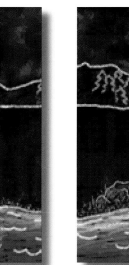

The entire landscape of Kaleida's *Playfarm* was too big to load onscreen at once. Therefore, we broke it up into tiles of a manageable size that ScriptX could piece together onscreen as needed.

ONLINE DESIGN

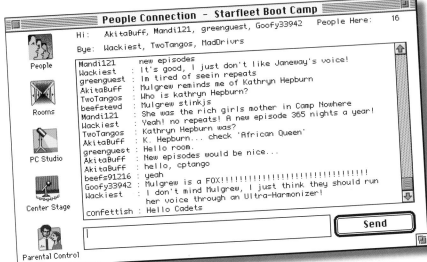

You can design a Web site's graphics to change over time, whether to offer limited sales opportunities or to simply reflect the time of day.

One of the fastest-growing areas of multimedia design is online design for sites on the World Wide Web (WWW). No longer is multimedia limited to CD-ROMs and other delivery media. Though both multimedia and online design share many of the same needs, techniques, and strategies, such as user interface, resolution, and color palettes, there are some important differences.

ONLINE STRENGTHS

There are a few attributes that are unique to online multimedia: time, community, associative links, and convenience. When designing an online site, try to maximize these areas since they are, in essence, what define this new medium.

TIME

Once a CD-ROM is pressed, it cannot be updated. The information, in effect, is set in stone. Web sites, however, can be updated daily, or hourly, if need be. Therefore, think of time as a creative element of your design. For instance, imagine a Web site with graphics that change to reflect the time of day. Or imagine an online store featuring a "one-day-only" sale.

COMMUNITY

The architecture of the World Wide Web supports immediate, cheap, and widespread dissemination of information. It is also highly democratic. As easily as a big corporation can have a Web site, you, too, can have a personal Web site that people from all over the world can access.

ASSOCIATIVE LINKS

Because most Web addresses are long, obscure sequences that no one could possibly remember, a large part of the interactive experience comes from linking from one site to the next. "Net surfing," as it is referred to, is often an associative process.

For instance, by looking for information on a trip to Hawaii, I came across a link for Kona coffee. Clicking on the coffee link brought me to a coffee store where I could buy the Kona coffee. There, I saw a link for the design company that created the site, and so I clicked to go there. As you can see, the cycle can go on and on as long as there are links at each site.

Anonymity is very popular in the online community. In the "chat rooms" of America Online, users from all over the country can meet and exchange ideas without knowing each other's true identity. People often assume fanciful names and free themselves from their normal inhibitions. Because such community forums are unique to the online world, designers should consider including them as part of their designs.

Therefore, unless there is a business reason not to, it's important to provide links to other sites.

CONVENIENCE

The above factors of time, community, and associative links give online multimedia a convenience that other media don't have. While sitting at home, people can have access to all kinds of information twenty-four hours a day. You can even buy food and have it delivered to your house the next day!

ONLINE LIMITATIONS

Along with all the benefits that online multimedia provides, there are limitations that affect designers. Currently, there are a number of browsers available, and they feature

varying degrees of graphic capabilities. (Browsers are applications like Netscape, Mosaic, and America Online's Web browser that allow you to "browse" the World Wide Web.) Because the browsers have varying graphic capabilities, Web sites are often designed for the lowest common denominator.

Modem speeds are another issue that designers must face. Most consumers are not equipped with a fast modem, let alone an ISDN, T1, T2, or T3 line (these provide relatively fast access to the Internet, enabling graphics and information to download quickly). Therefore, graphics for Web sites should be kept small in terms of file size so that they do not take too long to download over slower connections.

KidSoft has developed an electronic shopping catalog on America Online that allows users to browse through kids' software, see screen shots, read additional information, and even download demos. Users can also buy the software online.

DESIGNING A WEB SITE

In designing the PowerTV Web site, we decided that the home page would be one large graphic that would link to six places. Though it is full-screen, this image compressed down to only 30K while retaining quality. This is because we extensively used flat color areas and limited the use of photographic images.

Before creating a Web site, you should be familiar with the design constraints of today's online technology. Listed below are thirteen issues to consider.

1) FILE SIZE

Designing Web sites is analogous to designing for the static page. Currently, animation is very limited, and building complex structures and virtual environments is slow and difficult. Therefore, you most often hear people talking in terms of Web "pages." Web pages can be as long as you design them to be, but only so much can fit in the browser's window before users will need to scroll down. Try to compress the graphical contents of any individual page to under 100K, preferably to 50–60K or less. The smaller the graphics' file sizes are, the faster they will download.

2) FILE COMPRESSION

Since online speed can be a problem, try to make graphics as small as you can in terms of their file size. Two file formats, GIFF and JPEG, compress graphics files for use on the Internet. The GIFF file format compresses graphics the most because it works only with 8-bit images. But keep in mind that the GIFF format does not compress photographic-like images very well. Flat color, on the other hand, compresses extremely well in the GIFF format. Therefore, try to keep a balance of complex and flat imagery (see example shown at left). The JPEG file format works only for 24-bit images. Consequently, JPEG images will be larger than GIFF images.

3) SCREEN DIMENSIONS

Because most consumers have 13" monitors, it's a good idea to design Web pages to fit within that space. But the actual area you have to work with is even smaller than the 640 x 480 pixels of a 13" monitor. This is because the interface functions of most browsers, like Netscape, take up a lot of screen space. Therefore, the actual screen dimensions before users have to scroll down to see more are about 485 pixels wide x 350 pixels high.

4) NO GRAPHIC LAYERS

HTML (HyperText Markup Language) is the programming language used to create Web sites. It is a fairly simple language that has limited graphic capabilities. One of its limitations is that it does not allow layers of graphics; only one graphic can occupy space at a time. This is why animation and graphical feedback (such as highlight states), are limited on the World Wide Web.

5) VERTICAL FLOW

On Web sites, all graphic and textual elements are stacked up vertically one after the other; no two elements can be side by side. For instance, you cannot have an image on the left side of the screen with text that wraps on the right. To do this, you need to create a graphic banner as wide as the screen that contains the graphic on the left and graphic text on the right.

6) LEFT ALIGNMENT

Browsers align graphic elements and text to the left. A few browsers give you the control to align text in various ways, but

Since PowerTV would be updating the content of each of the six places, we developed simple "masthead-like" banners to run across only the top of the pages.

The structure of the Lopuck Media Design site is a flattened hierarchy. Each of the five banners lists links to the other four places, making navigation easy (see "Flattened Hierarchy" on page 22).

keep in mind that some consumers' browsers will not support anything but left alignment. There is a way to make graphics appear centered by using a transparent color as a "place holder" (see Number 12, "Transparency," below).

7) TYPOGRAPHIC CONTROL

There is a limit to the control you can have over text formatting. While you can specify the point size and the font, end users will need to have that font available on their computers in order to see your design correctly. Therefore, to be safe, it's best to choose a standard font. The way to get around this limitation is to use graphic text. Be aware, however, that graphic text will take longer to download.

8) ISMAP (INVISIBLE HOT SPOTS)

Many Web sites use "hot text" as the interface that links you to various pages. If you want to use a graphical interface, however, HTML has a feature called "ISMAP" that can draw invisible hot spots over various areas of a graphic. For example, if your interface consists of graphics alone, the way to make certain areas "hot" is to use ISMAPs.

9) NAVIGATION

Most browsers allow users to turn off the graphics to save downloading time. Therefore, you should always provide a text-based way of navigating a Web site in addition to a graphical interface.

10) COLOR PALETTES

Most Web-site graphics use an 8-bit color palette, but you can always cut down on file size by using fewer colors, such as 6-bit or 5-bit color.

11) BACKGROUND COLOR AND TILES

Web browsers usually have a default background color. Netscape, for instance, uses a gray background. Keep in mind that you can specify any background color you like, or you can set up a small pattern that is tiled across the background. (Graphics placed on top of a tiled background are not considered an additional layer.)

12) TRANSPARENCY

Much like a key color in multimedia, you can make one color of an online image transparent. Using a transparent color is a way to get around the left-justification rule. Create a banner the length of the screen using one solid color that will become transparent. Then center your image on the banner.

13) VRML, HOT JAVA, DIRECTOR, AND MTROPOLIS

The limitations of today's authoring tools for the WWW are quickly becoming a thing of the past. Soon, virtual spaces and extensive animation will be possible on the Internet because of new tools like VRML (Virtual Reality Markup Language) and Hot Java (a new Web-site authoring tool). In addition, multimedia authored in tools like Director and mTropolis will be able to "play" online.

The home page of Lopuck Media Design establishes a user interface based on color and shape to identify categories. Though content is always changing, the categories remain constant and are reinforced visually.

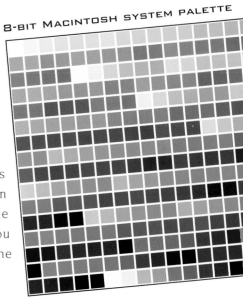

8-BIT MACINTOSH SYSTEM PALETTE

TOP 10 PRODUCTION DOs & DON'Ts

Now that you're familiar with the multimedia graphic production process, here's a handy checklist of dos and don'ts that you can refer to as both a reminder and a guide.

1) USE 640- X 480-PIXEL SCREEN DIMENSIONS

Most consumers today own small 13-inch monitors. Therefore, in order to reach a large audience, both multimedia and online applications should be designed within the screen size of this monitor, which is 640 pixels wide and 480 pixels high (about 9" x 6.5") .

2) USE 72-DPI RESOLUTION

Computer monitors are generally built to display a fixed resolution of 72 pixels per inch. Because of this, graphics created for multimedia and online purposes should be 72 dpi so that there is a one-to-one mapping of image resolution to monitor resolution. Be sure to work in 72 dpi, too—there is no need to work on images at a higher resolution and then scale them down to 72 dpi when you finish editing them. During the editing stages, it is better to see the image as it will actually appear.

3) KEEP GRAPHIC ELEMENTS IN SEPARATE LAYERS

Multimedia is a dynamic, ever-changing environment. Images are constantly fading in and out, animating across the screen, and changing into new images. To maximize these dynamic capabilities, it is best

BLUE SCREEN TECHNIQUE

to keep all graphic elements as separate files. Think in layers. Do not combine graphic elements that you intend to animate into the background graphic.

4) SAVE LAYERED ELEMENTS SEPARATELY

The Photoshop layering feature allows you to create separate graphic elements together in one Photoshop document. This feature allows you to get a sense of how your images inter-relate yet enables you to keep them separate from one another. Authoring tools, however, will not read this layered Photoshop document. In the end, you will need to disconnect all the layers and save them separately.

5) USE ALIASED EDGES FOR KEY COLOR IMAGES

If you intend to key out the background color surrounding a graphic, remember that only one solid color can become transparent. If your image has been anti-aliased to the key color, the blended outer edges of the image will not be dropped out and will remain as a rim of artifacts. Therefore, be sure to use aliased edges for key color images.

6) USE ANTI-ALIASED EDGES FOR OVERLAYS

If a graphic overlay will not be moving across the background (or if the background will not be changing underneath it),

ALIASED EDGE   ANTI-ALIASED EDGE

then it is safe to combine the graphic to a cutout portion of the background. This way you can create an overlay that retains anti-aliased edges.

7) REMEMBER: MULTIMEDIA GRAPHICS ARE BITMAPS

Many designers ask if they can use their Illustrator EPS files in a multimedia project. The answer, at least today, is no. All graphics for multimedia and online applications must be converted to bitmaps. Bitmaps are graphics that are defined by a collection of pixels, or dots of color. Photoshop, however, can read Illustrator files and convert them from vector-based illustrations (graphics defined by a series of mathematical points and curves) into bitmapped illustrations. This conversion process is called rasterization—Photoshop rasterizes graphics from Illustrator.

8) SAVE A COPY OF FINAL GRAPHICS IN 24-BIT COLOR

Always save a copy of your final graphics in 24-bit color (see page 102). You never know when you will need to refer back to them, such as when a client wants changes. You never want to make major changes to an 8-bit graphic because you will be limited in terms of the palette and will have to simulate by hand the "dithering" (a pointillism-like way of visually mixing colors). Also, if you need to make prints of your work, it's best to print from 24-bit versions.

9) REDUCE EACH IMAGE'S PALETTE TO 8-BIT COLOR

When you are through preparing images and have saved them as separate files, the last thing you need to do is reduce their palettes to 8-bit (see page 102). Reducing the number of colors used in your images from millions to 256 significantly enhances the speed at which the computer can display the images on the screen. Also, most consumer monitors are not capable of displaying more than 256 colors at once, so there is no point in including wasted colors. You can use the Macintosh system palette, a Windows-compatible palette (see "Cross-Platform Palettes," page 113), or a custom palette, but be sure to use the "diffusion dither" method of arranging pixels (see pages 104–105).

ONLINE NOTE: Often, 8-bit graphics take too long to download in online multimedia. Try reducing your images to 6-bit or even 5-bit by using an adaptive color palette (see Exercise 5, pages 106–107).

10) SAVE IMAGES AS PICT OR BMP FILES

Authoring tools will only accept images saved in the PICT (for Macintosh) or BMP (for Windows) file formats.

ONLINE NOTE: Web-site and other online graphics should be saved as GIFF files. Some Internet browsers also read JPEG files, but for the most part, GIFF is the standard file format. The GIFF format takes up less disk space and thus it travels significantly faster over the network.

CHAPTER 6

UNDERSTANDING
COLOR & PALETTES

Just as traditional fine artists have an intimate understanding of the way pigments and surfaces work together, multimedia artists must have an understanding of the way color works on a computer screen. Knowing how computers use color and palettes will enable you to make better design decisions about their use.

The use of color is one of the most critical and trickiest design issues in multimedia. It can be used to connote importance, specify categories, direct the eye, reflect a mood, or establish style. The challenge is to decide how many of these things color can be all at once.

—Kristee Rosendahl, Modular Arts

PAINTING WITH LIGHT

TRADITIONAL PRINTING TECHNIQUES

In order to reproduce color images on paper, they must first be separated into just four colors: cyan, magenta, yellow, and black (CMYK). Each color is screened through a grayscale "stencil," or plate, so that it is imprinted on the paper at various strengths. The buildup of these four colors, at various strengths, reproduces a wide range of colors. This same principle is used to produce images on the computer screen, but instead of painting with ink, it paints with light.

RED, GREEN, AND BLUE LIGHT

Computer monitors display color by blasting various intensities of red, green, and blue light into the space of one square pixel. The fullest intensity of all three colors overlapped together in one space creates pure white.

Just as in nature, all colors of the spectrum together create white light. It is not until light is refracted through water or a prism that we see all of the colors individually, as in a rainbow. On the other hand, the absence of the three colored lights creates black.

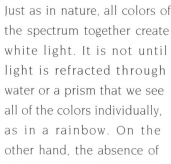

256 COLOR INTENSITY LEVELS

Imagine painting a grayscale from pure white to pure black using 256 increments. Now imagine that you were to use this grayscale as a stencil to silk-screen a color onto a surface.

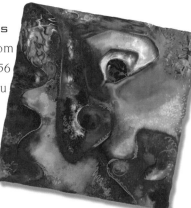

In a subtractive color process, as in the case of printed color, white is achieved by the absence of color—the subtraction of color. Four plates, or "screens," allow cyan, magenta, yellow, and black ink to pass through at various dot sizes. The larger the dot, the more intense the color.

When painting with light, true white is achieved by adding all colors together. This process is referred to as additive color. Notice the three "screens" that red, green, and blue light pass through at various intensities to produce a multicolored composite.

As a stencil, the gray value now represents the intensity through which color can pass. Pure black blocks color completely, while pure white allows color to pass through completely (at 100 percent). The gray values in between screen color at various percentages.

Computers use a scale consisting of 256 levels of intensity for each of the three additive colors: red, green, and blue. Therefore, there are 256 "reds," 256 "greens," and 256 "blues" to work with. With all these reds, greens, and blues, you can create over 16 million colors (256 x 256 x 256).

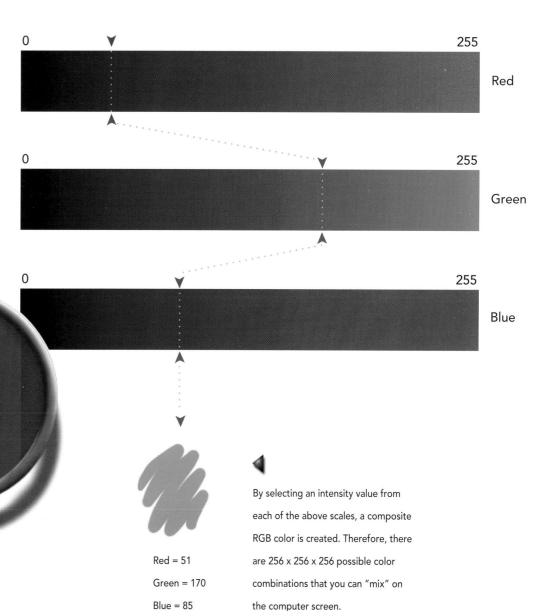

0   255

Red

0   255

Green

0   255

Blue

A close-up reveals the 256 incremental steps on the intensity value scale.

Red = 51

Green = 170

Blue = 85

By selecting an intensity value from each of the above scales, a composite RGB color is created. Therefore, there are 256 x 256 x 256 possible color combinations that you can "mix" on the computer screen.

Color Depth

24-BIT COLOR DEPTH

Though the computer's RGB color system is able to create millions of colors, it takes computer processing power to display them. In order to display all 256 intensity levels of one color (red, green, or blue), 8 bits of computer information are required. Thus, in order to display all three intensity scales, 24 bits of computer information are needed.

Unfortunately, most consumer computer configurations do not come with enough VRAM (video random access memory) to display 24 bits worth of color (millions of colors) on the screen at one time. While some can display 16-bit color (thousands of colors), most stock computers can display only 8-bit color (256 colors).

16-BIT COLOR DEPTH

When a computer has only 16 bits to display color, rather than showing you all the possible mixtures of just two colors, say red and green, it distributes the possibilities evenly across all three colors. Therefore, at any one time, the computer can display about 65,000 combinations of red, green, and blue (256 x 256).

The same image is shown here at three different color depths: 24-bit (top), 16-bit (middle), and 8-bit (bottom).

8-BIT COLOR DEPTH

Having 8 bits of computer information for color limits the onscreen display to only 256 combinations of red, green, and blue at one time. Since most consumer computers can only show 256 colors, multimedia graphics should be reduced into an 8 bit-palette (see page 102) in order to reach the largest audience.

WORKING AND SAVING IN 24-BIT COLOR

An image can be saved at any of the above color depths. However, it's best to work with 24-bit images (in Photoshop, the "RGB mode" is 24-bit) and save originals as 24-bit images. Otherwise, you are limiting yourself during the creative process. Only after an image has been completed and is ready to be integrated into a multimedia application should you reduce the color palette from 24-bit to 8-bit.

A Photoshop alpha channel works like the above address stencil. By spray-painting through the cutout, or mask, you can paint your address on any number of objects. Thus, not only can you control which area gets painted, but you can also use stencils over again to reproduce the cutout shape. In the above example, the stencil (mask) is like a Photoshop alpha channel and the objects are like Photoshop layers.

32-BIT COLOR DEPTH

If there are only three colors, each with 256 levels, creating the computer's color spectrum, and it takes 24 bits of computer information to display all possible combinations at once, then what is a 32-bit image? It's an image that has a fourth, 256-step, grayscale "plate," or alpha channel, associated with it. When you save an image as a PICT file in Photoshop, a dialog box offers you the ability to save it as a 32-bit image (to save its fourth alpha channel, too). A fourth alpha channel does not affect the coloration of an image; instead, it serves as a mask (shown at right).

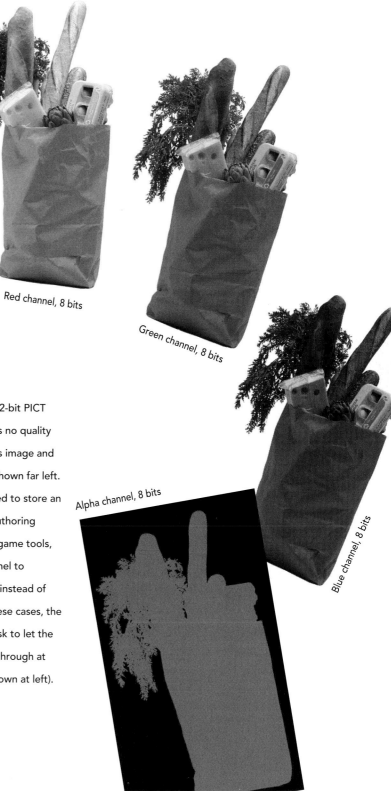

32-bit image

Red channel, 8 bits

Green channel, 8 bits

Blue channel, 8 bits

Alpha channel, 8 bits

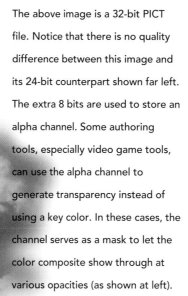

The above image is a 32-bit PICT file. Notice that there is no quality difference between this image and its 24-bit counterpart shown far left. The extra 8 bits are used to store an alpha channel. Some authoring tools, especially video game tools, can use the alpha channel to generate transparency instead of using a key color. In these cases, the channel serves as a mask to let the color composite show through at various opacities (as shown at left).

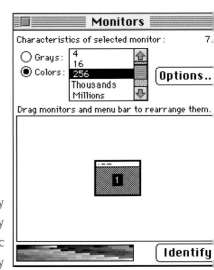

EXERCISE 4
EXPERIMENTING WITH COLOR DEPTH

This experiment demonstrates the effects that a monitor's color depth has on the quality of images. In this exercise, we will compare various color-depth settings by changing the Macintosh's monitor control panel. (This exercise only works on Macintosh computers capable of supporting 24-bit color.)

STEP 1

Before you get started, first be sure your monitor is set to 24-bit color. (Often, if you are using multimedia programs, your monitor will be automatically set to display 8-bit color.) To do this, choose Control Panels from the Apple menu. Within the Control Panels, open the Monitors panel.

STEP 2

In Photoshop, open a 24-bit, fairly detailed image that uses a wide variety of colors. For the most dramatic results, choose an image that not only has a lot of colors, but that also features gradients of color.

STEP 3

With the image opened in Photoshop, go back to the Monitors panel and position the panel side by side with the Photoshop image (so you can see the results).

STEP 4

Switch the color depth in the Monitors panel to millions of colors, thousands of colors, 256 colors, and even 16 colors. Notice how the 24-bit image "remaps" its use of color according to the monitor's setting.

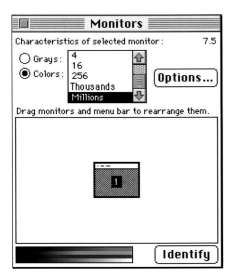

To find out the color depth your monitor is capable of, open the Monitors panel, located in the Control Panels under the Apple menu. If your computer has enough VRAM, you will be able to scroll beyond the 256-color setting and set your monitor to thousands or millions of colors.

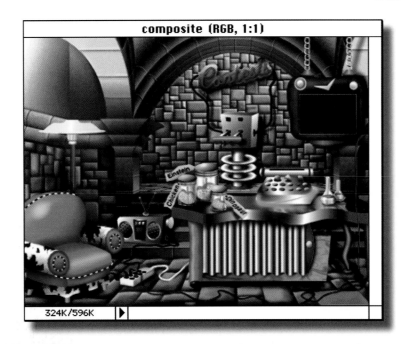

When creating the KidSoft Clubroom, I worked in 24-bit color even though the final art needed to be indexed (see page 102) into an 8-bit color palette. This allowed me to have maximum control during the creative process. For instance, if the monitors were set to a lower color depth, it would be difficult to see the fine details while illustrating the reflections on the tabletop.

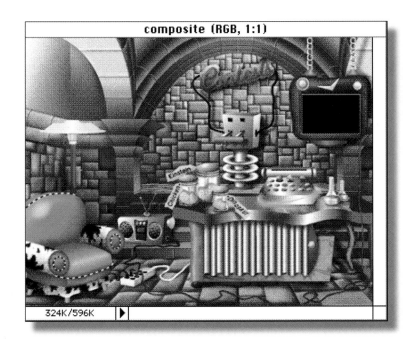

composite (RGB, 1:1)

324K/596K

Notice how the 24-bit image shown below left appears to have a strange burlaplike pattern imposed on it when the monitors are set to an 8-bit color depth. This is the standard dithering method used by 8-bit displays (see "Dithering Methods," pages 104–105).

To see an extreme example of how the monitor's color depth affects an image, try setting the monitor to a 16-color display (different from a 16-bit display, which displays thousands of colors). Notice that the bottom of the Monitors panel shows you which colors it is using to display images on the screen.

CONCLUSION

Many designers complain about the poor quality of onscreen graphics. This simple exercise, however, points out that poor quality is not always the fault of the image and that it's important to check the color-depth capacity of your monitor before you begin working.

Imagine trying to edit the 24-bit image at right while viewing it forced into the monitor's standard 8-bit, 256-color palette. Regardless of the monitor's setting, an image can still contain 24 bits of color information. Therefore, in order to see what you are doing, you need to have the monitors set at the highest possible color depth, preferably 24-bit, but 16-bit is generally OK, too.

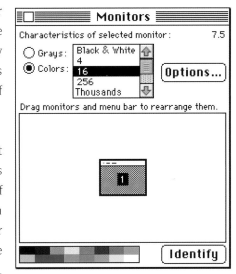

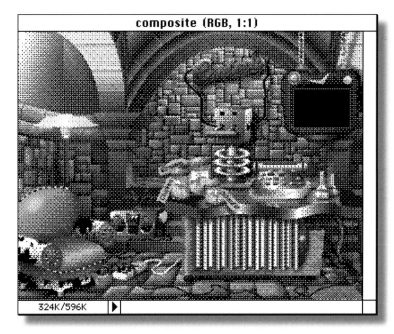

composite (RGB, 1:1)

324K/596K

C₆LOR PₐLETTES

CONTINUOUS-TONE IMAGES

Before a color photograph has been separated into four color plates for printing, it is a continuous-tone image—meaning that it consists of dots of all colors instead of combinations of only four colors arranged in various sized dots. A 24-bit image is essentially a continuous-tone image because the image has access to millions of colors if it needs them.

Unfortunately, the added information associated with a 24-bit image takes up a lot of disk space and creates drag on the system, making users wait. Also, most consumer computers cannot display all of the colors contained within a 24-bit image and will force the image into a standard set of 256 colors. For these reasons, 24-bit images are almost worthless in a multimedia context; they need to be reduced into an 8-bit palette of 256 colors.

INDEXING AN IMAGE

The process of reducing the number of colors in an image from millions (24-bit color) down to only 256 (8-bit color) is called indexing. Once an image has been indexed into a limited color palette, there is no going back, even by changing the mode back into 24-bit. The process discards color information and then emulates the discarded colors by juxtaposing two or more similar colors.

For instance, if the indexing process threw away the oranges and recreated them by using reds and yellows, simply changing back to a 24-bit color depth will still leave you with red and yellow pixels; the computer will not remember the oranges that were once there. Therefore, always save a copy of your 24-bit originals.

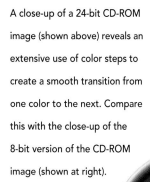

A close-up of a 24-bit CD-ROM image (shown above) reveals an extensive use of color steps to create a smooth transition from one color to the next. Compare this with the close-up of the 8-bit version of the CD-ROM image (shown at right).

The same CD-ROM image is now limited to a standard palette of only 256 colors. Of these colors, only a few are appropriate for this particular gradation. By strategically interspersing a few colors, the gradation is approximated—albeit with a pointillistic look.

Compare the 24-bit image at left with the 8-bit image at right. Since the 8-bit palette does not have the correct orange, yellow and red pixels visually "mix" to create it.

HOW PALETTES WORK

A collection of 256 colors are stored in a "color look-up table" (CLUT), a 16 x 16 square grid. Each of the 256 squares on the grid is given a unique address, numbered from 0 to 255, so that the computer and the image can reference them. An RGB color value is then assigned to each square.

Onscreen pixels are indexed to one of the numbered squares within the grid. For instance, the orange used to color the wing of the butterfly in the image shown at left is stored in square 18. If you go into the color palette and alter the color of square 18, say to navy blue, then the areas of the image that reference square 18 will now change to blue, as shown in the image at right. As you can see, the location of the square within the grid is important—images reference the address of the square, not the color within it.

Where colors are located within this grid becomes an important detail when developing cross-platform palettes (see page 113) and when using palettes to animate images (see "Color Cycling," page 112).

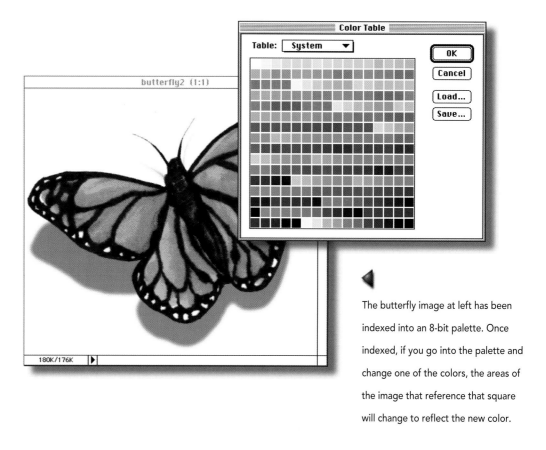

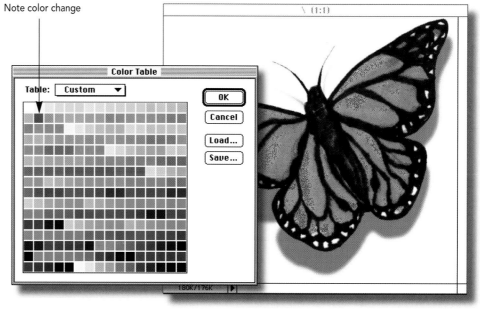

The butterfly image at left has been indexed into an 8-bit palette. Once indexed, if you go into the palette and change one of the colors, the areas of the image that reference that square will change to reflect the new color.

Note color change

Custom Palettes

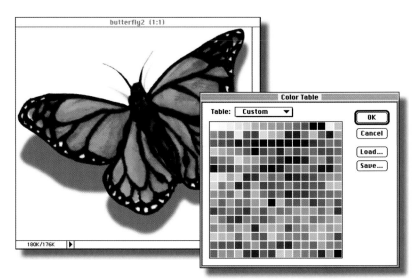

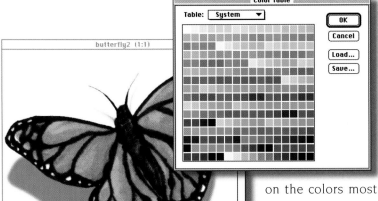

When reducing 24-bit images down to a limited palette, there are a few palette options and strategies to consider. You can either choose to use a standard palette, like the Macintosh system palette, or you can create a custom palette based on the colors most used by an image or series of images. Also, you can choose between two different methods of arranging pixels when dithering images into a limited set of colors.

This butterfly image has been indexed into the Macintosh system palette. Notice that there are a lot of colors, such as greens and blues, in the palette that this image does not need. Therefore, the image is further limited in its choice of appropriate colors.

STANDARD 256-COLOR PALETTES

Both Windows and Macintosh have a standard collection of 256 colors (called the Windows default palette and the Macintosh system palette) that do a good job of representing most images. But because standard palettes have been designed to accommodate a wide range of colors, they produce average results overall.

When using a pre-composed set of colors, chances are there will be a lot of wasted colors. For instance, yellows, purples, and reds will probably not be needed in a seascape image. Those unused colors take up slots in the color table that could otherwise be filled with more shades of blue.

CUSTOM PALETTES

Therefore, in order to get optimal results, you need to create a custom palette composed of the 256 colors that best suit a particular image. In Photoshop, you can do this by creating an "adaptive palette," one of the options found in the Indexed Color function under the Mode menu. DeBabelizer can also create adaptive palettes.

DITHERING METHODS

Much like traditional pen and ink drawing, where one color is used to visually suggest a tonal range, dithering is the process of using a limited number of colors to visually "mix" a wider range of colors. For example, by strategically juxtaposing a few colors, such as dots of yellow and red, the eye perceives orange.

Dithering, as you might imagine, tends to give images a pointillistic look. While using a custom palette minimizes the pointillistic effect, there is no way to avoid it completely. There *are* ways in Photoshop, however, to control the method in which images are dithered. Just as cross-hatching and stippling are two different ways to create the illusion of

The same butterfly is shown here indexed into a custom palette. Compare this palette to the generic Mac system palette and notice the near-24-bit quality of this image as a result.

tone with one color, there are two different dithering styles available in Photoshop: the diffusion dither and the pattern dither.

The diffusion dither is a more natural, random arrangement of pixels whereas the pattern dither is much more rigid, creating a burlaplike pattern over an image. The pattern dither is the method used by computers that can only display 8-bit color. That is why I recommend avoiding the pattern dither—it makes your work look as though the monitor is controlling the dither. Besides, in my opinion, the diffusion dither does a better job of "mixing" colors.

ONE PALETTE ONSCREEN AT A TIME

While you are running in 8-bit mode, you can never use more than one 8-bit palette onscreen at a time. Having two palettes of 256 colors exceeds the limitations of an 8-bit monitor's display capabilities. When there are two images onscreen that each have their own color palette, the image that is active, or on top, takes precedence. The image underneath gets remapped into the dominant image's color scheme. When the bottom image comes to the top again, its palette then becomes dominant.

This diagram shows the various computer methods used to display images as they compare to traditional drawing techniques.

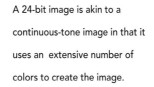

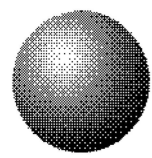
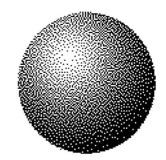

A 24-bit image is akin to a continuous-tone image in that it uses an extensive number of colors to create the image.

An 8-bit color image using the pattern dither method looks much like the cross-hatching technique used in pen and ink drawing.

The same 8-bit image using the diffusion dither method looks like the stippling technique used in pen and ink drawing.

EXERCISE 5
CREATING CUSTOM PALETTES

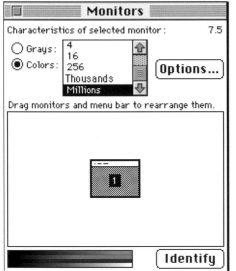

First set your monitor to display 24-bit color. This will allow you to view two images with different palettes at the same time.

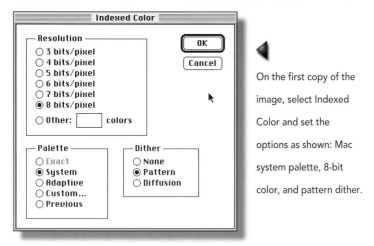

The following exercise leads you through the process of using Photoshop to reduce a 24-bit image into three different palette and dithering combinations. By viewing these three side by side, you can compare the various results. (For this exercise, you will need Photoshop and a Macintosh with a monitor that can display 24-bit or 16-bit color.)

STEP 1

Make sure that your monitor is set to the highest color depth that it can support.

STEP 2

For the most dramatic results, open in Photoshop an image that contains a wide range of colors and that also contains color gradients. From now on, I will refer to this image as the "original."

STEP 3

Make three copies of your original and arrange them around the screen so that you

For best results, choose an image that has a wide variety of colors and that includes gradients of color.

On the first copy of the image, select Indexed Color and set the options as shown: Mac system palette, 8-bit color, and pattern dither.

can see all four images next to each other. (If you have a smaller monitor, use smaller images so that you can see all four at once.)

STEP 4

Keep the original a 24-bit image as a basis for comparison and select the first copy to reduce into a palette. In Photoshop, under the Mode menu, select the Indexed Color option. This brings up an intermediate dialog box in which you can specify a palette and dithering strategy.

For this first example, select 8-bit color depth, system palette, and pattern dither. (Note that this is the default palette and dithering strategy that the Macintosh uses when it is set to 8-bit color depth.)

STEP 5

Select the second copy and again, under the Mode menu, bring up the Indexed Color dialog box. Choose 8-bit color and system palette,

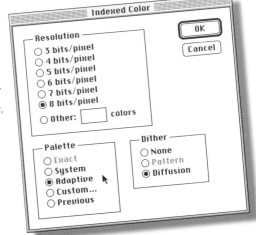

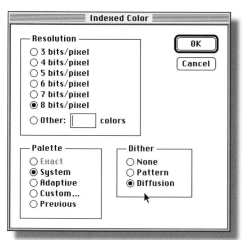

On the second copy, again choose the system palette and 8-bit color settings. This time, however, choose diffusion dither.

but this time choose the diffusion dither method instead of the pattern dither. Notice that although the image is mapped into the same set of colors (the system palette), the diffusion dither strategy alone gives you very different results.

STEP 6

For the third copy, we will create a custom 8-bit palette adapted to the colors used in the image. Select the Indexed Color option again, and in the dialog box, choose 8-bit color. This time, however, instead of choosing the system palette, choose the adaptive palette, which creates a custom palette adapted to the colors in your image. The diffusion dither is automatically selected when you set up an adaptive palette.

CONCLUSION

With all four images onscreen, compare the quality of the three copies that have been reduced in palette to the original 24-bit image. Looking at the first two copies that adopted the system palette, I recommend the one that uses the diffusion dither. Though the third image looks closest in quality to the original, there are palette management issues associated with using custom palettes (see pages 112–113).

The last copy of the image will be indexed into a custom palette. Select the adaptive palette option and 8-bit color. Diffusion dither is automatically selected for adaptive palettes.

Original 24-bit image   8-bit, system palette, pattern dither

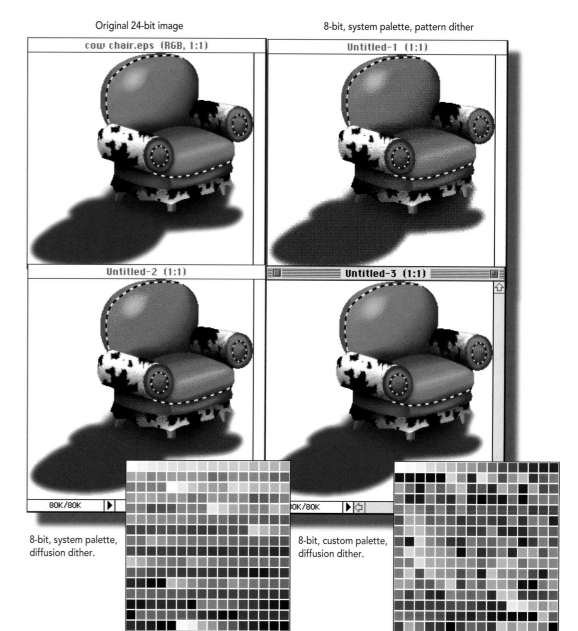

8-bit, system palette, diffusion dither.

8-bit, custom palette, diffusion dither.

Compare the copy with the custom palette to the copies that use the Mac system palette.

SUPER PALETTES

Because of the palette management issues (see pages 112–113) associated with using a different custom palette for each image, it's best to use as few palettes in a multimedia title as you can. But since custom palettes produce such nice results, you can gain the benefit of custom palettes while using only one or two palettes in a title by creating super palettes.

Just as it is possible to create a custom palette that consists of an image's most-used 256 colors, it is also possible to create a custom palette that has been optimized for a series of images. This is called a super palette.

BEST USES

Super palettes are only worthwhile, however, when the series of images share a similar color scheme. Factoring in a series of images that has a wide range of colors results in a super palette no better than the generic Mac or Windows system palette. In fact, both the standard Macintosh and Windows system palettes are essentially super palettes that were probably created by factoring in thousands of images. The wider the range of colors, the less the palette can specialize.

CREATING A SUPER PALETTE

The easiest way to create a super palette is to use DeBabelizer. DeBabelizer can read through a series of graphics and figure out a palette of 256 colors that best represents the group. It then creates a custom "super palette" and proceeds to dither the images into that palette. All this is done in one big automated sequence.

You can also create a super palette in Photoshop by copying and pasting representative parts of your images into one

Above are images from three different "ages" in Cyan's *Myst*. Notice that all the graphics of each age were designed with the same hues and tonal qualities. Each age uses its own super palette.

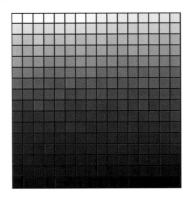

Because these images vary wildly in color, the resulting super palette is less than optimal. There are a lot of colors in the palette that are not needed by the individual images.

large Photoshop document. Then create a custom adaptive palette, save it, and proceed to apply it to your series of images. This route, however, is less reliable because only small representative samples get factored into the palette.

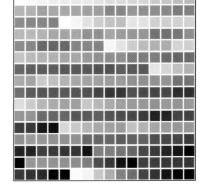

These images share similar colors and tones. Therefore, a super palette created from them will yield good results because each of the images can make good use of the selected 256 colors.

The same set of images shown above here uses the standard Mac system palette. Even though the super palette created above was less than optimal, it is still better than using a standard Mac or Windows system palette.

EXERCISE 6

CReATING A SuPER PαLETTE

This exercise takes you through the process of creating a super palette in DeBabelizer. For the best results, find a set of images that share a similar color scheme, such as a series of muted-color nature scenes. (Note: This exercise is geared for Macintosh computers.)

STEP 1

Create a new folder and place your series of images into it. When using DeBabelizer, it's easiest to store all the images to be processed within one folder. Not only does this make them easy to find, but DeBabelizer also has a way of adding all the contents of a folder into its "to do" list at once, saving you the trouble of placing images into the list one by one.

STEP 2

Open DeBabelizer. Under the File menu, select Batch. Batch has a pull-down menu; choose Super Palette from it. This brings up the window shown at left.

STEP 3

The first thing you need to do is create a new list of images to process (click New… in the upper left corner). In the dialog box

that appears (shown below), select and open the folder containing your images. In the middle column of buttons, select Append All. This creates a Batch List in the right column. Below that, enter in a name for your list, and click Save.

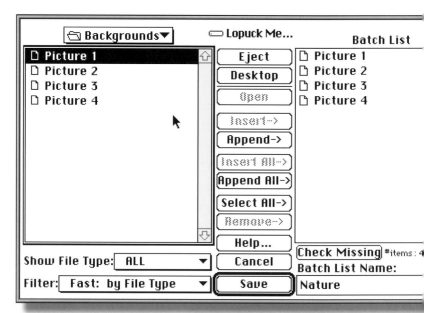

STEP 4

Once you have created a list, you are brought back to the Batch SuperPalette window and are all set to go; just click DO IT (shown at left). When DeBabelizer is through (which takes just a minute), it shows you the proposed super palette (shown at right); click Create It.

Once you set up your list of images to process, click DO IT to factor the colors of your images into a super palette.

The four images shown across the top of these pages are the ones I used to create the super palette below.

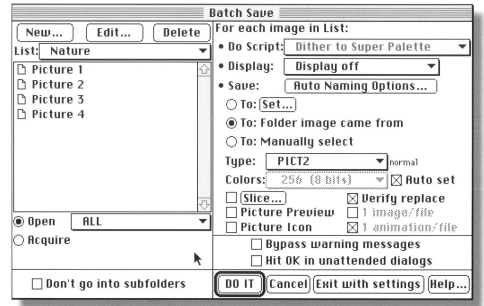

STEP 5

Once DeBabelizer creates the super palette, you are left with no open windows. At this point, you have only created the super palette; now you have to tell DeBabelizer to dither and save your set of images into the palette. Under the File menu, select Batch and under Batch, select Batch Save.

STEP 6

The Batch Save window that appears (shown at right) should still have your list stored in the left column. Now all you need to do is select the Dither to Super Palette script in the Do Script pop-up menu (located in the right column). On the bottom of the window, click DO IT. DeBabelizer automatically dithers the list of images into the super palette and saves them.

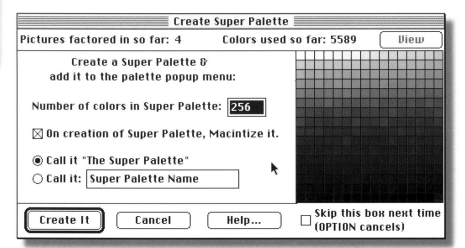

Create Super Palette

Pictures factored in so far: 4   Colors used so far: 5589   [View]

**Create a Super Palette &
add it to the palette popup menu:**

Number of colors in Super Palette: [256]

☒ On creation of Super Palette, Macintize it.

◉ Call it "The Super Palette"
○ Call it: [Super Palette Name]

[Create It]   [Cancel]   [Help...]   ☐ Skip this box next time (OPTION cancels)

Batch Save

[New...]   [Edit...]   [Delete]

List: [Nature ▼]

🗋 Picture 1
🗋 Picture 2
🗋 Picture 3
🗋 Picture 4

◉ Open [ALL ▼]
○ Acquire

☐ Don't go into subfolders

For each image in List:

• **Do Script:** [Dither to Super Palette ▼]
• **Display:** [Display off ▼]
• **Save:** [Auto Naming Options...]

○ To: [Set...]
◉ To: Folder image came from
○ To: Manually select

Type: [PICT2 ▼] normal
Colors: [256 (8 bits) ▼] ☒ Auto set

☐ [Slice...]   ☒ Verify replace
☐ Picture Preview   ☐ 1 image/file
☐ Picture Icon   ☒ 1 animation/file

☐ Bypass warning messages
☐ Hit OK in unattended dialogs

[DO IT] [Cancel] [Exit with settings] [Help]

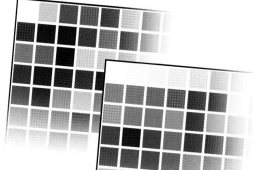

PaLETTE STRATeGIES

ORIGINAL 8-BIT IMAGE

BRIEF COLOR FLASH

SETTLED INTO NEW PALETTE

PALETTE FLASHING

The problem with having more than one palette in a multimedia title is transitioning from one palette to the next. When switching images onscreen that use different palettes, there is a brief flash when all colors change wildly. This unsightly phenomenon, which I call palette flashing, is caused by a new set of colors inserting themselves into the color look-up table (the 16 x 16 square grid). When a new color gets inserted into a square on the grid, the image areas referencing that square will briefly remap to the square's new color before finding a more appropriate color elsewhere in the new palette. As you can see, the location of colors within the grid is an important detail (shown below).

COLOR CYCLING

There is a way, however, to take advantage of the flashing of colors when palettes change. By creating two or more palettes that are identical except for a few colors changed in certain squares, only the image areas that reference those nonidentical squares will change when the palettes are cycled through on the screen. Therefore, by simply changing palettes behind the scenes, you can animate colors of an image in a controlled manner. This is called color cycling. For example, if you have an image of a fire that you would like to animate, you can change just the reds, oranges, and yellows in a series of palettes. Then, when the palettes cycle through, the fire will appear to flicker. Just make sure that the colors you are cycling are not used in any areas of the image that you do not want to flash.

DEVELOPING A SET OF PALETTES

Even though you can have only one palette in use on the screen at one time, there is nothing to prevent you from developing a few different palettes, each optimized for the color scheme used in a different section of a title. Cyan's *Myst*, for example, uses a different super palette for each of the "ages" of the game. In general, however, problems arise when transitioning from one palette to the next.

SMOOTH PALETTE TRANSITIONS

When you are not using palettes to animate an image, but just need to load in a new palette, you need to take certain steps to avoid color flashing (shown above). The way to do this is to identify a common color used in the same location in both palettes. If you notice, all palettes, whether standard or custom, use white and black in the first position, 0, and the last position, 255. (Macintosh palettes default to white in the first position and black in the last, while the reverse is true in Windows palettes.) After fading out all colors except for black or white, you can change palettes without flashing and then fade up the new colors.

Though drastically different, these two palettes position black and white in the same location. Therefore you can fade out all colors except for white or black, change palettes without color flashing, and fade up the new set of colors.

Some authoring tools, such as Director, allow you to fade out all the colors of a palette (fade out the image) leaving just pure black or pure white. Then, since palettes generally have white and black in the same location on the color look-up table, you can switch palettes without a color flash. The rest of the colors of the new palette are then faded up. This transition technique is known as "fade to white" or "fade to black."

Imagine that this image of a fire used a palette of only nine colors. By creating three variations of its palette, changing the color arrangement on each one, you can create a three-state flickering animation.

CROSS-PLATFORM PALETTES

In order to develop a suite of graphics that will work on both Macintosh and Windows platforms, you have to create a custom palette that addresses both of their needs.

MACINTOSH VERSUS WINDOWS PALETTE

The Macintosh system palette has white in the first position, 0, and black in the last position, number 255. But the Macintosh is not picky about this arrangement; the system is happy as long as black and white are in the first and last slots on the color look-up table. Windows, on the other hand, requires that black be first and white be last. Also, Windows requires a specific arrangement and color value for the first ten and the last ten positions in the color palette. Therefore, in order to make cross-platform graphics, you need to create a custom 8-bit palette that conforms to the Windows requirements. (See Exercise 8, 116–117.)

Windows requires that the first ten and the last ten positions in the color palette be organized as follows:

EXERCISE 7

PALETTE FLASHING

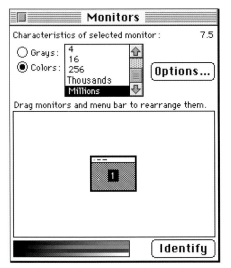

Before starting this exercise, set your monitor to display 24-bit color. This way you will not notice the color flashing until later in the exercise when we set the monitor to 8-bit color.

This exercise uses Photoshop to demonstrate the effects of palette flashing—showing you what happens when two images, that have different palettes, are on the screen at the same time. (Before beginning this exercise, set your monitor to 24-bit or 16-bit color, following the directions outlined in Exercise 4 on pages 100–101).

STEP 1

Choose two images that are nearly opposite in color scheme, and following Exercise 5 on pages 106–107, create an 8-bit custom palette for each.

STEP 2

Now that you have created a custom palette for each image, position both images side by side onscreen.

STEP 3

While the monitors are set to 24-bit or 16-bit color, you should be able to click back and forth between the two images without noticing any color flashing.

STEP 4

Set your monitor to display only 8-bit color and return to Photoshop. Switching back and forth between the two images now reveals undesirable color flashing effects that occur in poorly planned multimedia titles. Notice that the foremost image (the active window) becomes the dominant palette, remapping the images underneath into its palette. The images not in the active window briefly reflect the new color and then quickly re-index themselves to the new color set. Such an uncontrolled flash of colors alarms the user and lends an unprofessional tone to a multimedia title.

IMAGE AND CUSTOM PALETTE

Position both 8-bit custom palette images side by side onscreen in Photoshop.

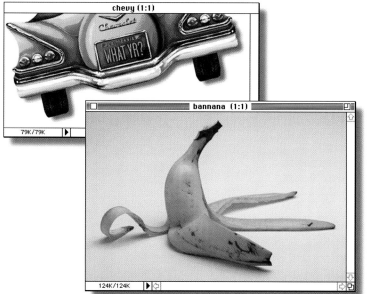

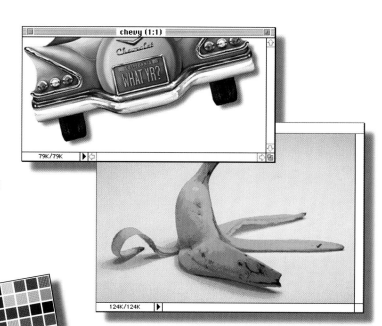

Since the banana image is active, its palette takes precedence over the car's palette. The car is remapped into the banana's palette.

IMAGE REMAPPED INTO NEW PALETTE

2

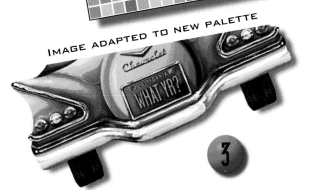

IMAGE ADAPTED TO NEW PALETTE

3

Each color of an image is indexed to a certain square in the CLUT (color look-up table). When a new palette loads onscreen, it most likely has a different color assigned to that square. The image area is briefly filled with the new color until it finds a more appropriate color in a different square. This brief moment of remapping produces color flashing.

EXERCISE 8
CROSS-PLATFORM CUSTOM PALETTES

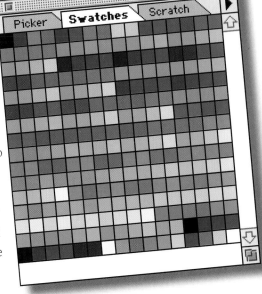

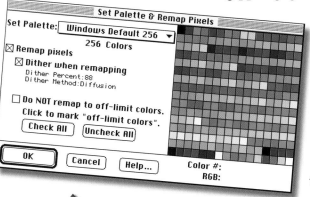

The first step in creating a custom cross-platform palette is to open any image in DeBabelizer and change it into the Windows default 256-color palette. Any image will do because you need only the palette.

In order to create custom palettes, including super palettes, that will enable your graphics to work on both Macintosh and Windows computers, you will need to arrange the first ten and the last ten colors in a specific way. This exercise uses Photoshop's Palette window to piece together colors from the Windows default 256-color palette and colors from a custom palette to arrive at a cross-platform custom palette.

STEP 1

One way to create a custom palette that uses the colors in the right locations is to start with DeBabelizer. Open an image in DeBabelizer and under the Palette menu, choose Set Palette and Remap Pixels. A window appears within which is a Set Palette pop-up menu. This gives you a number of palette choices; choose the Windows default 256 palette and click OK.

STEP 2

Once the image has been remapped into the Windows palette, save the image and quit DeBabelizer. (A window

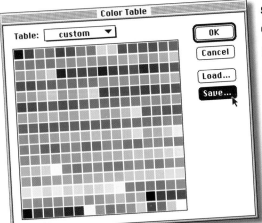

In Photoshop, open the DeBabelizer image that has the Windows default 256-color palette. Open its Color Table (located under the Mode menu) and save it by clicking the Save... button.

will appear asking you to "Macintize the Palette," which would switch the white and black color positions; ignore this and click OK.) Open the image in Photoshop.

STEP 3

Now that you have the image saved in the Windows default palette, you need to separate it into its first and last ten colors. In Photoshop, under the Mode menu, choose Color Table. You will see the Windows palette appear in the window. Choose Save…, give it a name, and save it in a convenient place (I always save it on the Desktop). Then, under the Photoshop Window menu, choose Palette: Show Swatches and load the saved Windows palette into the Swatches. To do this, click on the upper right arrow (which has a pull-down menu) and choose Load Swatches. A dialog box appears and asks you to locate a palette. Locate the saved Windows palette and click Open.

STEP 4

In the Swatches window, delete all colors from the Windows palette except the first ten by holding down the Command key while clicking on the other color squares. When you are through, save this color set by choosing Save Swatches from the upper right arrow's pull-down menu. Name it "First Ten."

Add the saved Windows palette to the Swatches window by clicking on the upper right arrow and choosing Load Swatches.

STEP 5

Load in the original saved Windows palette again, as in Step 3. Repeat Step 4, but this time delete all colors from the Windows palette except the last ten. Save this color set as "Last Ten." Save the "First Ten" and the "Last Ten" color palettes for later; you will use them at either end of your custom palette.

STEP 6

Create an 8-bit adaptive palette or super palette for your image (see Exercise 5, pages 106–107, or Exercise 6, pages 110–111). Go into the Photoshop Color Table window (located under the Mode menu), choose Save…, and give this palette a name.

STEP 7

If it's not there already, load the "First Ten" color set into the Swatches window by choosing Load Swatches from the upper right arrow's pull-down menu. Then add your custom palette into the Swatches window by choosing Append Swatches from the upper right arrow's pull-down menu. Finally, Append the "Last Ten" colors.

STEP 8

You now have twenty more colors loaded into the Swatches window than you are allowed in an 8-bit palette (256 colors from your custom palette plus the twenty from the first and last ten Windows default palette colors). You need to look at the colors inside your custom palette and delete twenty of them that look like

First, delete all colors from the Windows palette except for the first ten by holding down the Command key and clicking on the colors. When you are done, choose Save Swatches from the upper right arrow's pull-down menu. Call it "First Ten."

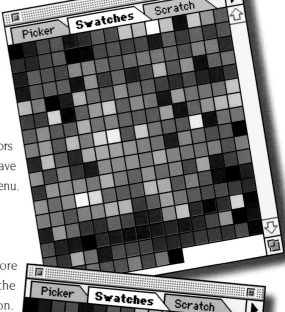

duplicates or that are similar to colors elsewhere in the palette. Delete these colors by holding the Command key down and clicking on them (the same way you deleted colors in Steps 4 and 5). Two easy colors to delete are the extra white and black that were included in your custom palette.

STEP 9

Once you have honed the palette down to 256 colors in the Swatches window, save it by choosing Save Swatches from the upper right arrow's pull-down menu. Give it a name and save it in a convenient location.

STEP 10

Open a copy of your original 24-bit image (before you indexed it into a custom palette). Under the Mode menu, choose the Indexed Color option. In the dialog box that appears, choose the Custom… setting and click OK. When the Color Table appears, click the Load button. A dialog box asks you to locate a palette. Find the cross-platform palette you pieced together in the Swatches window and click Open. Then click OK in the Color Table, and your image will be remapped into your cross-platform palette.

nteract

HNMS, HE WATCHES AND FEELS

+ (Sürf)ace

.com/is/?not?ith

VOICE
212.533.4467

ilo 360°
digital design

FACSIMILE
212.533.4578

133 West **19**th Street | Th3d Floor NEW YORK | **NY** | **10011**

PRESS
forward

ilo

H□ME

H□ME

G
ALLERY

Information Acce
a Multi-Dime
Interaction

John Davis
Richard Ba

Cranbrook Academy of A

CHAPTER 7

MEDIA DESIGN
SHOWCASE

Visual designers have long complained about the limitations of designing for the computer screen: the resolution, the screen size, etc. These limitations have often been the reason designers have steered away from interactive multimedia altogether. But increasingly, designers are bridging the gap and are raising the visual standards of multimedia. This last chapter shows six examples of how designers have contributed to both user interface and visual design in multimedia.

An interactive experience is a three-way relationship between users, authors, and machines—each must have a say for the relationship to grow. In the best designs, control of the experience flows back and forth between all participants, like a good conversation.

—Fabrice Florin, Zenda Studio

I/O 360 DESIGN

The I/O 360 Design Web site is a combination of client work, experiments, and work in progress that together communicate an evolving approach to design and content creation in the digital realm. The overall visual design is integrated with the site's internal user interface structure. All content-related elements are laid out evenly in a "flattened hierarchy" so that any part of the site is easily accessible from the other parts. The site, while acknowledging the essential page metaphor of standard Internet browsers, seeks ways to subvert this metaphor by freeing pages from a traditional grid layout and by breaking up the linearity of the user's experience through its flattened structure.

http://www.io360.com/

▶

Scenes from the *I/O 360 Interactive Agent* and other design works are available by clicking on the "experiments" button (shown below left). This agent-based interface is discussed on pages 58–59.

B

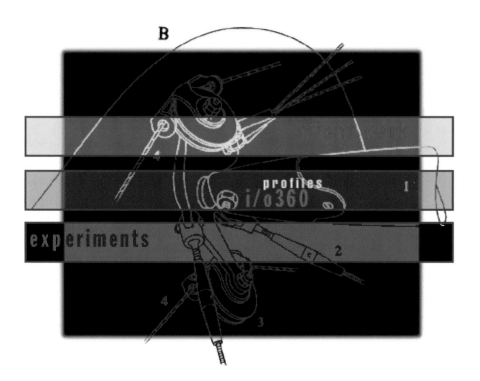

profiles
i/o360

experiments

133 W 19TH · THIRD FLOOR · NEW YORK NY 10011
(2 1 2) 5 3 3 - 4 4 6 7

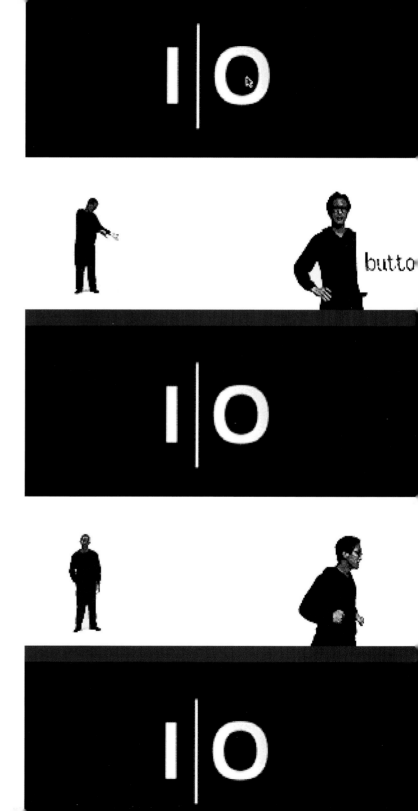

AMERICAN CENTER FOR DESIGN

Interact, a combination CD-ROM and book, is the 1994 edition of an annual journal published by the American Center for Design. The journal presents a collection of exemplary user interface design ideas in a medium that suits the content—interactive multimedia. From a single front-end interface (which in this case is a map larger than the screen so that users need to pan around), users can choose which design example to view by clicking on schematic-like line drawings peppered around the map. Each abstract drawing represents a different design example.

Information.Environment
8vo

interact

▲

When you first start *Interact*, the above banner appears and then quickly flashes the words "click me" accompanied by a voice saying the same words. If the user does not respond, the banner flashes and darts around the screen accompanied by a louder voice prodding the user to "click me."

John Davison   Richard Bates

J K L M N O

Information
Access

Cranbrook Academy of Art

By clicking and holding the cursor down on one of the abstract drawings on the main interface, text appears that identifies the design example it represents—in this case, "Information Access" (shown at left). To get to the design example, double-click.

▼

One of the design examples included in *Interact* is *Information Access*, an integrated software and hardware interface solution for searching information that was developed by John Davison and Richard Bates. Like using a magnifying glass, users move the above screen closer to objects in order to get more information on them.

Information Access—
a Multi-Dimensional
Interaction

John Davison
Richard Bates

Cranbrook Academy of Art

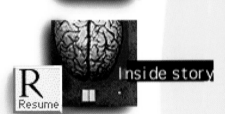

DAN DESIGN

Noah Dan calls himself a "one-person design empire." His Web site displays an eclectic assortment of his work, ranging from a design portfolio to artwork to illustrated recipes. His design style is, in a sense, reactionary. It stands in contrast to the "technology worship" style prevalent on the Web. He achieves an organic look by carefully using backgrounds and shades. The end results are screens that contain not only buttons and information but also a warm atmosphere.

Web design

What's cooking

...a little cyber trip?

MAIL →

Gallery

Resume

Inside story

Illustratio

Art Dir.

Advertisi

http://www.digimark.net/dan

The design of a graphical main interface screen presents a set of problems. The most notorious issue is the speed at which the images download. The remedy is a careful balance of compression, format, size, and color depth. The JPEG-format interface screens are kept below 85K. As they draw, they "peel off" the more captivating images first, to keep the viewer's interest until the screen is drawn in its entirety.

"The only way for an artist to make decent money is to develop a unique style," my father used to tell me. By now I know I'm not going to make "decent money," not in this incarnation, not on illustration. I don't have the discipline to limit myself to a set of tools and materials nor the patience to develop a style. I get all hot and bothered by new materials and techniques, ...hell, one thing for sure, it's never a dull moment.

illustration

Gallery

Links

BASTIDE & BASTIDE

The French design firm Bastide and Bastide designed *The Maeght Foundation: A Stroll in 20th Century Art*, a CD-ROM "walk-through" of the Foundation's art collection. The interface starts off with a circular video window that shows a "walk-through" point of view. As the video passes a work of art, an icon of the work appears onscreen. If the user rolls over the icon with the cursor, the icon turns into a caption that identifies the work. As the video progresses, more icons of artwork appear onscreen. As the screen fills with new icons, older ones fade off to make room. To get more information on one of the works of art, simply click on its icon.

ENTRANCE GARDEN

Once you click on an artwork's icon, you are brought to a close-up of it along with its accompanying information. Icons of similar or related works of art appear in a vertical scrolling palette. Clicking on one of these icons brings you to its corresponding close-up. General navigation functions such as "go back" are stored in the vertical black bar on the left of the interface.

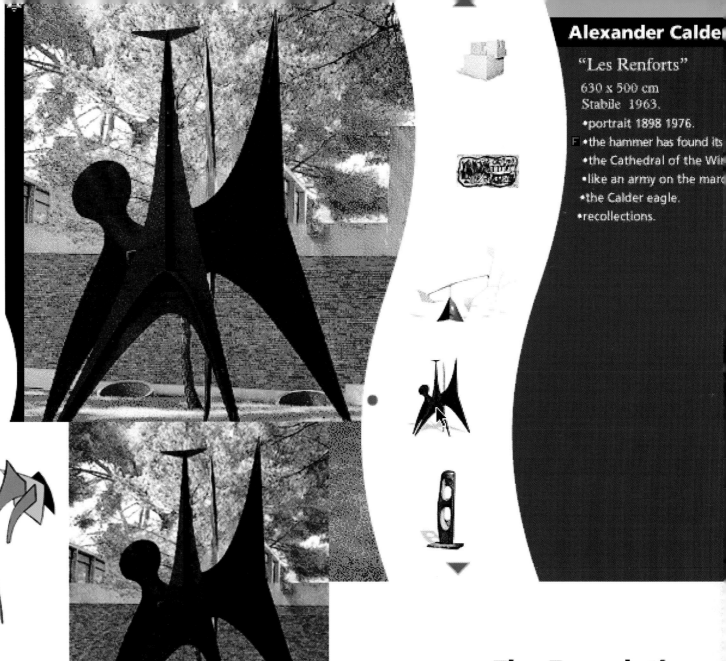

Alexander Calder

"Les Renforts"
630 x 500 cm
Stabile 1963.
- portrait 1898 1976.
- the hammer has found its
- the Cathedral of the Win
- like an army on the marc
- the Calder eagle.
- recollections.

The Foundation
Marguerite & Aimé
Maeght

a stroll in 20th century art

Executed specially for the Foundation, "Les Renforts" is incorporated in the architectural model of a Mediterranean

ANNIE SHAPIRO

WE MAKE MEMORIES

ABBE DON

In this CD-ROM developed by Abbe Don, a pictorial timeline of her family photographs that date from 1890 to the present enables viewers to move through time on the computer screen to hear the story of her family's history, culture, and assimilation into American life. Don used her great-grandmother's storytelling style as a model of interactivity to reveal how her family history has been passed down matrilinearly for four generations. Viewers hear family stories and cultural critiques such as the role of women in Jewish families and the changing status of women and education through time.

To move foward and backward through time, users simply move the cursor to the far right and far left of the screen until the cursor changes into a pointing hand, then click and hold down the mouse to scroll through time. By clicking on the four women (inset in the four corners of the interface), users can access the point of view of four generations.

1890 1900 1910 1920 1930 1940 1950 1960 1970 1980 1990

▼ BELOW IS THE ENTIRE TIMELINE SPANNING 100 YEARS OF THE FAMILY'S HISTORY.

2MARKeT

GIFT
selections

2Market is a CD-ROM shopping catalog that features a wide variety of products from over 25 well-known stores such as Lands' End and The Nature Company. Introduced in 1994 and designed and developed by Medior, 2Market is a beautifully designed example of multimedia used for sales purposes. Not only does it satisfy the functional needs of electronic shopping, but it also provides an easy-to-use, inviting user interface.

GIFT 2MARKET SHOPPING

CLICK ON GUIDE TO PLAY MOVIE

GIFT *ideas*

find a gift

GIFT REMINDER

GO TO   HELP   CALL (800) 622-6600 TO BEGIN YOUR 2MARKET SUBSCRIPTION.

2MARKET

MESSAGES

CATALOGS, RETAILERS & MORE

COLLECTIONS

GIFT SHOPPING

FIND

YOUR SELECTIONS

CALL (800) 622-6600
TO BEGIN YOUR 2MARKET SUBSCRIPTION.

When you first launch 2Market, music starts as your video host walks onscreen in front of the graphical interface, introduces you to 2Market, and explains its interface. You have the choice of either the "Collections," which brings you to a list of all the companies to browse; "Gift Shopping," which helps you find a gift for someone; "Find," which helps you find a particular product; and "Your Selections," which is where the products you select are stored.

personal
SELECTIONS

Squiggle Ball   Finger Boiler Pen

The Collections button on the main interface screen takes you to a submenu that provides links to the various "storefronts." The storefront shown at left is The Nature Company. By clicking on one of the departments listed on the right, users enter the store and start shopping for products (shown above). Each store has been designed within a template so that there is a consistent user interface from one store to the next.

APPENDIX

Successful interface designs are the result of an iterative process, constantly shaping the design to meet users' needs, accommodate technical or budget limitations, create a compelling aesthetic experience, and in the case of multimedia, let the content emerge clearly and directly without navigation and gimmicks getting in the way.

—Abbe Don, Abbe Don Interactive

Getting A First Assignment

Where to look

When you are just starting out, the best way to get familiar with multimedia and online companies is to look through multimedia magazines and write down the names of companies in your area that interest you. Magazines often publish "awards" issues highlighting the "top ten" CD-ROMs or Web sites; these issues usually include screen shots, so you can get a sense of each company's design needs and direction. The magazines usually list names of people to contact at each company, too. Be sure, however, to identify the actual developer of the product and not the publisher, because the developer is the person who would require your services. Finally, build a database of developers and make a note of their style and their products before you start calling them. You make a stronger impression when you are informed about a company and its products.

Internships and volunteering

Unless you are lucky, you are going to have to get practical experience in multimedia before you get your first assignment. A good way to do this is to volunteer your design skills to a multimedia development company or to find an internship. Many multimedia developers are small and operate on equally small budgets, so they are usually happy to get free help from talented designers. Internships may be unpaid, but if they do pay it may be only $7–$9 an hour.

Do it yourself

If you cannot spare the time to either volunteer or work as an intern, you might consider creating your own multimedia applications. If you can think of ways to augment your current work by creating multimedia presentations, then you can start to build a multimedia portfolio *and* impress your clients at the same time. For instance, if you are creating a package design for a client's product, you can create an interactive presentation that displays your different design directions and shows how the product might look in various settings. The disadvantage to this approach is that you will not build the multimedia developer contacts that you would by volunteering or by interning.

Networking

Contacts in this industry are everything! Choose your mentors wisely and get involved in as many multimedia "Special Interest Groups" (SIGs) as you can—especially when you are first starting out. Although it is growing, the multimedia community is a small one and everyone either knows each other or has worked together on a project. Now is the time to get established; the friendly climate may change as the industry matures and more money starts changing hands.

SALARIES & FEES

Most designers want to know how much multimedia designers are charging for consulting work and what kind of full-time salaries they are commanding. Because there are more designers in the print industry than there are in the multimedia industry, and because multimedia has a more technical nature, multimedia designers of all skill levels are generally paid twice that of their print colleagues.

CONSULTING FEES

The following fees are averages for intern-level, entry-level, mid-level, and high-level multimedia designers. Designers just out of school with some experience in multimedia can expect $12–$20 an hour. With some polish and practical experience, an entry-level designer can charge about $25–$30 an hour. Mid-level designers, who have worked on a variety of multimedia projects and have a solid understanding of the production issues and processes, can charge $35–$45 an hour.

Experienced designers, who are known in the industry, and who are very good, can charge $50–$100 (or more) an hour. Experienced designers offer a lot more than creative services—they can facilitate a title's creative production, foresee engineering and structural problems, design top-notch user interfaces, and coordinate the design talent.

FULL-TIME SALARIES

Full-time salaries, as a rule, are about 75 percent of consulting fees when spread out over a year. For instance, if you charge $60 an hour, a ballpark full-time salary for that level would be about $75–$80K a year. This is because of trade-offs like job stability, benefits, equipment that you no longer have to buy, annual bonuses, and stock options. Overall, graphic design positions in multimedia companies range from $35K a year for entry-level designers to about $80K a year for experienced art directors to about $100K (or more) for experienced creative directors. Of course there are always special circumstances, and fees and salaries will vary in different parts of the world.

ROYALTIES

The big trap for designers, and other service-oriented people, is that unless you can arrange an equity stake in the companies and the products you do design work for, you are forever doomed to only selling your service hours. Since there are only so many hours in a week to sell and only so much you can charge per hour, your financial growth is limited.

It is not unheard of for designers to share in the ownership of a title; after all, it is usually the creative direction that plays a big part in the title's success. Sometimes it makes sense to lower your hourly fee in exchange for equity because of the potential to collect much more once the title is in the marketplace.

SeLF-PROMoTION

Before venturing out as a multimedia designer, you need to develop your own identity program, complete with mailing materials, letterhead, and most importantly, a demo disk. Multimedia and online developers like to see a complete, well-thought-out portfolio that shows them your experience.

I have developed a suite of modular materials that I mix and match depending on the needs of a client. These materials consist of: a mini multimedia slide show that fits on a diskette and features screen shots of titles I have designed, a portfolio of color prints of screen shots, CD-ROMs of multimedia projects, "one-pager" mailing brochures (both electronic and printed), and a Web site that is always updated. The nice thing about showing your work on a diskette, a CD-ROM, or a Web site is that clients can see your work in the medium that it was designed for.

Every so often I have "one-pagers" made that reflect various styles of my work. The front displays screen shots and the back provides company information and a client list.

Design a modular portfolio system so that you can mix and match the color prints of your work. This allows you to arrange a collection that best appeals to the needs of each client.

BOOK RES_OURCES

Design Essentials
Luanne Cohen
Adobe Press
A visual guide to various production
techniques using Photoshop and Illustrator.

Director Demystified
Jason Roberts
Peachpit Press
A thorough overview, with tutorials, of Director 4.0
that gets you up to speed creating your own
multimedia titles. Includes CD-ROM.

Illustrator 5 for Macintosh: Visual QuickStart Guide
Elaine Weinmann and Peter Lourekas
Peachpit Press
A step-by-step guide to learning Illustrator.

Imaging Essentials
Luanne Cohen
Adobe Press
A visual guide to various production techniques using
Photoshop, Illustrator, and Premiere.

Multimedia Demystified
Apple Computer and vivid publishing
An overview guide to all aspects of multimedia, from
production, including team building and CD-ROM
mastering, to running a multimedia business.

The Photoshop Wow! Book
Linnea Dayton and Jack Davis
Peachpit Press
A practical step-by-step guide for learning intermediate
and advanced Photoshop techniques. Includes disk.

Photoshop Filter Finesse
Bill Niffenegger
Random House
An extensive guide to Photoshop plug-in filters that's
loaded with tips on creating various special effects.

Photoshop 3 for Macintosh: Visual QuickStart Guide
Elaine Weinmann and Peter Lourekas
Peachpit Press
A step-by-step guide to learning Photoshop.

Understanding Comics
Scott McCloud
Kitchen Sink Press
A thought-provoking look at graphical communication
design; a "must-have" for user interface designers.

CD-ROM RESOURCES

Buried in Time
Presto Studios
619-689-4895

The Cartoon Guide To Physics
Interactive Factory
617-426-0609

Club KidSoft
KidSoft
408-255-3434

Forever Growing Garden
C-Wave
415-397-3811

**Freddi Fish and the Case
of the Missing Kelp Seeds**
Humongous Entertainment
206-486-9258

Guides 3.0
Apple Computer
408-996-1010

The Incredible Machine
Sierra On-Line
206-649-9800

Interact
American Center for Design
312-787-2018

The Journeyman Project
Presto Studios
619-689-4895

**The Maeght Foundation:
A Stroll in 20th Century Art**
Bastide and Bastide
33-1-4527-4107

My First, Incredible, Amazing Dictionary
Dorling Kindersley
416-445-3333

Myst
Cyan
509-468-0807

Ocean Life IV: The Great Barrier Reef
Sumeria
415-904-0800

Quantum Gate
HyperBole Studios
206-441-8334

CD-ROM & ONLINE RESOURCES

2Market
2Market, Inc.
415-525-4700

The Tortoise and the Hare
Living Books
415-352-5200

Travelrama
Zenda Studio
415-777-9896

Voices of the 30s
Sunburst Communications
914-747-3310

Wacky Jacks
Zenda Studio
415-777-9896

We Make Memories
Abbe Don Interactive
Abbe@well.com

Wild Africa
Sumeria
415-904-0800

Xplora
Real World Multimedia
44-1-225-744-464

Dan Design Web site
http://www.digimark.net/dan/

I/O 360 Design Web site
http://www.io360.com/

KidSoft America Online site
Keyword: kidsoft

Lopuck Media Design Web site
http://www.LMDesign.com

PowerTV Web site
http://www.powertv.com

INDeX

C&LOPHON

This book was initially developed for a class I teach at the San Francisco State University Multimedia Studies Program, "Graphic Design: Making the Transition to Multimedia." It is because of the encouragement I received from students that this book is published today.

HOW THIS BOOK WAS CREATED

I wrote and designed this book in Quark XPress 3.3 on my Macintosh PowerBook 520c. My old faithful Quadra 700 and Photoshop 3.0 were used to process graphics and screen shots from multimedia titles into CMYK EPS files. Diagrams, illustrations, and decorative text elements were created in Illustrator 5.0. The two computers were constantly connected together to transfer graphic files from the Quadra to the PowerBook. The book was continually backed up on a Syquest 270-megabyte removable cartridge and finally archived on a CD-ROM.

Permission to recompose elements of multimedia titles for layout purposes was painstakingly sought in parallel to this book's development. At any one time, I was on the phone securing rights, faxing sample layouts to gain approval, and processing images!

FONTS

Chapter and individual page titles were set in a mix of Heliotype and Party. Subheadings and decorative type elements were set in Bank Gothic Medium. Book text was set using the Novarese family. Captions were set in Avenir Medium.

AB◉UT THE AUTHOR

Lisa Lopuck is a multimedia designer and illustrator who has put the creative face on a variety of interactive products for the educational and entertainment markets. Her design firm, Lopuck Media Design, specializes in the creative direction, user interface design, and production of interactive media and online applications. Prior to the formation of Lopuck Media Design, Ms. Lopuck was the Art Director of the Digital Media Group at KidSoft and the Art Director of the Media Design Group at Kaleida Labs, where she prototyped multimedia titles in ScriptX. She has consulted for a wide range of multimedia developers, including CKS Partners, vivid studios, Microsoft, PowerTV, the George Lucas Educational Foundation, Apple Multimedia Lab, and the Voyager Company. She is also a faculty member of the SFSU Multimedia Studies program where she teaches "Graphic Design: Making the Transition to Multimedia," "Beginning Photoshop," and "Intermediate Photoshop." Ms. Lopuck holds a B.A. in design from UCLA. She lives on the coast just outside of San Francisco with her husband and their two Akitas. She also has a horse, stabled nearby, and a dairy cow, who lives on a ranch in Idaho.

For more information on Lopuck Media Design, find the company on the World Wide Web at: http://www.LMDesign.com